Diary
of a
Bass Pro

A Year On the Inside
Of Fishing's Fast Track

By Joe Thomas with Tim Tucker

2/4/93

To Tim,

"Good Fishin"

A Tim Tucker Outdoor Production

BOOKS BY TIM TUCKER

Secrets of America's Best Bass Pros

More! Secrets of America's Best Bass Pros

Doug Hannon's Fisherman's Logbook

Roland Martin's 101 Bass-Catching Secrets

Advanced Shiner Fishing Techniques

To Ryan Joseph Thomas with the hope that he will have clean air, pure water and plenty of bass to chase in the future.

Published by
Tim Tucker Outdoor
Productions Corp.
Rt.. 2, Box 177
Micanopy, FL 32667

Printed in the United States of America by
Atlantic Printing
P.O. Box 67
Tabor City, NC 28463

Library of Congress Card Number 92-074447
ISBN Number 0-937866-38-5

Front and back cover design by Tom Scott Designs, Suite B-1506 McCallie Ave., Chattanooga, TN 37404 (615-622-1875).

Cover photo of Joe Thomas with the 1990 Red Man All American Championship check by Terry Freeland. Other photos by Tim Tucker, Diane Thomas and Gerald Crawford.

About the Authors

Joe Thomas became a fulltime bass pro in 1983 and since then has established himself among the top professionals in the country. After qualifying for three appearances in the prestigious BASS Masters Classic and the U.S. Bass World Championship, he enjoyed his greatest moment by winning the $100,000 top prize in the 1990 Red Man All American Bass Championship (the third time he had qualified for that crowning event).

His consistency on the national tournament circuit and ability to communicate have made Thomas an in-demand representative of fishing industry sponsors and seminar speaker. He is also a popular on-the-water fishing instructor.

Thomas, 31, wife Diane and son Ryan live in Mainville, Ohio.

Tim Tucker is one of the country's most published outdoor writers and bass fishing is his specialty. In addition to being a senior writer with *Bassmaster Magazine, Southern Outdoors* and *B.A.S.S. Times,* Tucker's work has appeared in *Field & Stream, Fishing Tackle Retailer, Southern Saltwater, Florida Sportsman, Florida Wildlife, Bass Fishing, Bassin', North American Fisherman, Fishing Facts* and numerous other publications.

Joe Thomas, left, and Tim Tucker study a lake map.

A longtime columnist for the *Palm Beach Post* newspaper, the veteran angler/writer has written six books books, including the popular *Secrets of America's Best Bass Pros* and *More! Secrets of America's Best Bass Pros* (Volumes I and II of the Bass Pro Series). This is the fifth book that his company has published.

His company also produced the *Bass Sessions*™ *Series* of instructional audio cassettes.

Tucker, 36, lives in Micanopy, Fla., with wife Darlene.

Table of Contents

Acknowledgements

There are several individuals who have played important roles in our personal and professional lives and we would like to publicly thank:

JOE THOMAS

To my wife Diane, my partner in every aspect of my life and career.

To my parents, Jim and Sabara Thomas, for their never-ending love and support. They've been behind me 100 percent from the beginning.

To my sponsors, past and present, for making my competitive fishing career possible.

To Ray Scott, for his personal interest in my career and also to his B.A.S.S. organization for taking this sport to its present plateau.

To fellow pro Rich Tauber, whose insight helped me take a hobby and turn it into a lucrative occupation.

To my family and friends for their encouragement since the very beginning.

Finally, I would like to thank God for giving me the ability to do what I do for a living.

TIM TUCKER

To Darlene, my biggest supporter, my source of inspiration and the nicest person on the planet, thanks for the last 14-plus years.

To Bob and Doris Tucker, for their wisdom and nurturing.

To Tom Mulligan, the most dedicated friend a person can have.

To friends and fellow professionals Gary Giudice, Mary Shelsby, Horace Carter, Richard Bowles, Mike Walker, Mark Thomas, Bob Dennie, Bob McNally, Wade Bourne, Gerald Crawford, Ann Lewis and countless others for their friendship both on and off of the water.

To editors Dave Precht, Matt Vincent, Colin Moore, Spence Petros and Larry Teague for their friendship and direction over the years.

To the bass pros as a group, who are mostly fine men and modern-day pioneers trying to make a living doing something that is every bit as difficult as trying to hit a major-league fastball.

To Rick Clunn, an inspiration more as a human being than as a fisherman.

To Gary Klein and wife Jana for setting an example of friendship, class and compassion that we all should follow.

To Roland Martin, for introducing me to this sport.

To Steve Moore and Gregg Harr, my longtime editors at the Palm Beach Post, for their confidence and support.

To Doug Hannon, for his friendship and the example he sets.

To Kim Rhodes, my editorial assistant, for her help on this book.

Finally, to the bass fans throughout America who enjoy and support the sport at both the professional and weekend levels. You are the most important people in the fishing industry.

Introduction

In more than a decade of covering the national bass circuits, you develop a sort of peripheral vision for a certain type of pro. The hard-charging up-and-comer. The eager guy on the outside looking in with an impatient confidence that he will soon move up to the next level. The guy whose life and career is consumed with reaching the pinnacle of the sport he has chosen to pursue.

That pretty well describes my first real memory of Joe Thomas.

As I look back, a youthful Joe Thomas seemed trapped within full view of the sport's sweetest rewards, but just beyond the reach of that brass ring. He had molded his young career into one worthy of notice, but try as he might, he just couldn't make the big jump — qualifying for the BASS Masters Classic, fishing's Big Show and the most important event in competitive fishing.

It seemed like every season since I became aware of his presence, the final tournament of the Bassmaster circuit would arrive to find Thomas on the verge of making his first appearance in the Big Show. That would be a pattern that would haunt his psyche throughout his career.

I vividly remember a scene from the final tournament in the 1985-86 season. I can still see Joe fighting back the disappointment, trying to keep his emotions in check well enough to project a positive image. And I can still hear B.A.S.S. founder and tournament announcer Ray Scott, with his Alabama drawl, consoling the 25-year-old pro, telling the crowd "Folks, this is a fine young man, the epitome of the All-American boy. It looks like he has just missed making this Classic. But he'll be back next year. I can promise you that. His best days are ahead of him."

I noted Scott's seemingly genuine affection for Thomas and offered him a word of consolation. But time would be his only consolation — in this case a year of days and nights.

It was with considerably more interest that I viewed Thomas' chances of making the 1987 Classic as the season wound down on Tennessee's Kentucky Lake. He had stayed on the fringe of the Classic standings throughout the year, but it came down to one final day. And the kind of pressure he had experienced 12 months earlier.

But on this day, fate and a helpful partner (veteran pro Jon Hall) would smile on Joe Thomas, allowing him to catch seven bass weighing an impressive 20 pounds, 15 ounces — and realize a dream. "Making the Classic was a goal of mine since I was 15 years old," he said that day.

That was when I really got to know the Cincinnati kid. In fact, I got to know him well enough to travel on the same emotional roller coaster that has been his career.

Thomas missed the 1988 Classic by a mere 9 ounces. He was only 4 pounds short of qualifying for the 1989 Classic. Each season, his Classic chances hinged on the final tournament, even the final day — a career trait he has learned to endure. In eight of his nine seasons as a professional bass angler, his Classic fate has come down to the last tournament. In four of those seasons, it was decided on the last day.

The summer of 1989 was the lowest point of a most promising career. Missing the Classic for the second consecutive year cost Thomas four of his eight sponsors — the lifeblood of any fishing career. Those sponsors dropped him despite the fact that he had always been among the best and most sincere promoters on the tour.

But Joe even managed to make the best of that situation, expressing his appreciation for those sponsors' support and hoping to work again together down the road. That's the class act I had learned to appreciate.

Thomas would regain several of those same sponsors the following year when he rebounded in impressive fashion. Not only did he qualify for his second Classic appearance, Thomas won one of biggest prizes in tournament fishing by winning the Red Man All-American Bass Championship during two fabled days on Lake Erie. Suddenly, he was on top of the fishing world and enjoying a view he had always dreamed about.

"I kind of redeemed myself in 1990 and my life changed dramatically," Thomas says today. "People began to believe I was for real. I was no longer just an almost-in-the-Classic kind of guy."

Indeed.

Since 1990, Thomas has established himself as one of the most consistent pros, qualifying for another Classic and doing well on several tournament circuits. No longer burdened by the weight of being a professional also-ran, Thomas has thrived at the sport's highest level.

It was in 1991 that Joe and I began discussing this book, fashioning a diary that offers an inside peek at this fast-track sport as well as a guide to catching more bass. Thomas was one of the few pros that I would consider involving in a year-long project in which he would be asked to bare his soul — share his vulnerability, failures and successes — into a tape recorder at the end of every tournament day of the 1991-92 season.

I have long admired James Joseph Thomas, the total package. He has molded and shaped his career into a model that any aspiring tournament pro should emulate. With Joe, image is everything, but not in the plastic, artificial way that tennis star Andre Agassi spouts off in the Canon commercials. Thomas has worked hard to maintain a clean cut, but warm and friendly image. A professional image. He can be a fisherman, a business man, a company spokesman or your best fishing buddy. It's a far cry from the tobacco-chewing, sloppy-dressing Bubba bass pro that has plagued the sport for years and has, largely, been responsible for it not attaining the same level of media coverage as golf and tennis.

People relate well to Joe Thomas because he is a class act.

There is no better candidate to write this book, regardless of how well or poorly he would perform during the 1991-92 season.

Joe Thomas with a bass that would make any 13-year-old proud.

Just consider the well-planned path his fishing career has taken.

It began with those early fishing trips, when Joe's dad, Jim, took him to Canada at the age of 10 or so. It continued when 13-year-old Joe walked the banks of various Ohio farm ponds catching yearling bass. The fishing fever reached a new level when he was hired by former Cincinnati Bengals receiver Chip Myers to work at his Bass Pro Shop at the age of 15. It was about that time that young Joe began to follow the exploits of Roland Martin and Rick Clunn — and think about making a living at the sport he loved so much.

"The only goal I had in life from the time I was 15 was to be a professional fisherman," Joe once told me.

When he was 16, the personable Ohio native bluffed his way into an invitation to join the Kingfishers Bass Masters of Southern Ohio. Actually, he lied, telling them that he was 18 and eligible to fish the club's tournaments. At 16, he fished his first two tournaments and ran face-first into the excitement of competitive fishing. The following year, Jim Thomas bought his son a bass boat and young Joe went on to finish in the top six of a 50-member club dominated by older, more savvy fishermen.

At 18, Thomas won his club's Mr. Bass award and represented his club in the state-wide B.A.S.S. event. His first real taste of winning came when he surprised the state's bass elite by capturing the Ohio B.A.S.S. Federation championship. Heady stuff for an 18-year-old.

From that point on, everything Thomas did was planned with a fishing career in mind. He first attended Ohio State University, studying fisheries biology. But he soon moved back home to save a little money, attend the University of Cincinnati (still pursuing a fisheries degree) and be able to fish more tournaments. The industrious young man went to school during the day, worked for the United Parcel Service at night and fished tournaments on the weekends.

After three years of consistent success in state and regional tournaments, Thomas entered his first big-league contest in 1983, a B.A.S.S. event held on Texas' Sam Rayburn Reservoir. Despite being a babe in these woods, he finished just out of the money — and his confidence soared. He fished the final tournament of the B.A.S.S. season in Wisconsin and won a boat in the traditional random drawing at the end of the event. The money he made from selling that boat funded his first full season as a bass pro.

In 1983-84, Thomas fished the entire circuit and recorded a couple of top 20 finishes. He came up less than 4 pounds short of making the Classic in his rookie season.

From that point, his career has progressed handsomely... three Classic appearances... three appearances in the Red Man All-American... qualifying for the U.S. Bass World Championship in 1986... cashing a check in nearly half of the B.A.S.S. events he's fished... eight top 10 B.A.S.S. finishes... more than $400,000 in tournament earnings... winning the 1990 Red Man All-American.

But more than just dollars and cents, and pounds and ounces, is the man that Joe Thomas has evolved into. He is appreciated by the outdoor press, his sponsors, fellow tournament pros and fishing fans everywhere.

I have enjoyed getting to know Joe better during the past few months and learning more about what makes him tick. I've enjoyed getting to know his wife Diane, a woman with top model looks and a big heart, as well as his family. I've enjoyed watching and hearing about the Thomas' preparation for their first child — including the time when Joe fainted while watching an explicit film on birth at his first child-birthing class (sorry Joe, but I couldn't resist reporting that piece of information).

And I enjoyed putting this book together, sharing Joe's highest and lowest moments over the past season. I am very happy to be able to present you, the reader and fishing fan, with an inside view of the professional fishing with its heroes and characters, pressures and pleasures, rewards and sacrifices — the world that has fascinated me for more than a decade. In the process, it is my hope that you will gain an insight into the big leagues of fishing and maybe even learn a few tips for catching more and bigger bass.

Bass wishes.

Tim Tucker
Micanopy, Fla.
Sept. 1, 1992

A new season begins — my 10th as a bass pro.

Chapter 1

Reflecting Back,
Looking Ahead

A new season, a fresh start

I'm coming off of two of the best years I've ever had. Obviously, that has increased my schedule tremendously. I've gone to 20 tournaments, which includes fishing both the B.A.S.S. Invitational and Top 100 trails, the Golden Blend Diamond Invitational circuit and the showcase tournaments like the Canadian Open and MegaBucks, along with other events.

Add to that another 45 promotional days this year and you can see that I've had a pretty busy year so far.

Today is a pretty important day for me. I'm pausing both to look behind me and try to look into the future. At this point in my career and personal life, I think this kind of contemplative time is important.

I just finished competing in the BASS Masters Classic, which was held in Baltimore and the Chesapeake Bay. The Classic is the most important event in competitive fishing. Qualifying for one of the coveted 41 spots in the Classic can solidify a career; winning the Classic can make you a millionaire and change your life.

The 21st Classic, my third appearance in the event, was disappointing for me, obviously. I finished 33rd and I had one day in which I zeroed in front of 10,000 people. That's a real humbling experience, but I'm kind of used to it at this stage in my career. You've got to take the worst with the best in this crazy profession.

I made a few mistakes in the Classic. First, I changed water the second day, opting to fish the grass instead of fishing the docks. My primary area was Middle River where I was flipping docks with a 4-inch ringworm and a 4-inch big black-and-blue crawfish around the docks and pier pilings. It was a pretty good pattern that produced some fairly decent fish there early. I caught four bass that weighed about 7 pounds the first day of competition.

I should have tried to stay with it. Instead, I tried to make something happen. Zell Rowland came in with that big stringer of more than 15 pounds — which everybody knew he caught in and out of the grass on a Pop-R.

I had located a very good grass line up on the north edge of the river. The problem was I chose the wrong day to go to it. It was bright, sunny, and calm — the worst day to fish grass. With that clear water the fish just wouldn't bite. I ended up blanking that day. In fact, I never had a bite all day.

So I went back to the Middle River the last day and caught four fish that weighed 5 or 6 pounds. I didn't stick to my game plan like I should have in the Classic.

My other mistake occurred while pre-fishing the Chesapeake before the pre-Classic off-limits period. During that time, I spent too much time looking at the water and not enough time fishing. At the time, I believed that the two months off-limits time significantly limited what I could learn from fishing during prefishing. So I spent most of my time learning my way around.

When the tournament practice started, Hurricane Bob came through, so we only got to practice one day instead of two. That is about a 7 1/2-hour day. I had to basically try and stuff two days of practice into one. Everybody had the same problem, but I handicapped myself by not fishing more two months earlier.

I won't forget this lesson — I will pre-fish hard for every Classic from now on.

After the Classic, my schedule allowed me just one day at my home in Mainville, Ohio (a suburb of Cincinnati). After cramming a lot into a single day, including packing my bags and getting my boat ready, I headed for Alton, Ill., to pre-fish for the first B.A.S.S. tournament of the 1991-92 season.

I have never been to Alton before and this part of the Mississippi River. I assumed that it would probably be a lot like the Ohio River, which is my home waters. I just wanted to learn my way around. I spent the whole first day on the upper end of the Mississippi River, fishing with a couple of locals, including Dave Leonard, a writer for Illinois Outdoors. Also in the boat was a local expert on that water.

They showed me the upper pool. I found a few sloughs that I really liked. I mainly concentrated on the backwater area, although I did look at some wing dams and things like that on the river.

From what I saw, the tournament, at that time, could be won running-and-gunning little spots on the main river. The bigger fish may come out of the backwater area sloughs. There aren't very many creeks on this pool of the river, so I had to really look hard for what creeks and backwater areas I was able to find.

I caught a pretty good limit the first day by running those backwater sloughs and flipping a 5-inch Gatortail worm. It was very hot. Ninety-five degrees — even the water was in the mid -80's. With the sun shining, the fish were tight to the cover. But, if you slowed down and flipped a lot of logs and laydowns in those backwaters, it wasn't too hard to catch a pretty good five fish stringer.

My dad joined me on the second day. I decided to look at the Illinois River. Everybody told me to stay away from the Illinois River because the fish are small and there aren't very many of them. With me, such advice usually makes me want to check it out for myself. It is probably a lot less pressured than the good areas where the local anglers all fish.

Spending the whole day in the Illinois River, I discovered that there is very little cover. It is a flat-type of river — very winding and kind of narrow in some spots. Very few creeks. Some sloughs but not very many. It consists mostly of main river-type fishing. Being raised on the Ohio River, I'm usually able to pick out the types of places where fish relate to current on the river systems.

I ended up catching a pretty nice limit of bass for this river — 6 to 7 pounds for five fish. And I had one get off that might of been a 2 1/2-pounder. The fish seemed to average 12 to 13 inches, which is very common in the river systems.

I caught better fish in the Mississippi. So I decided to spend my third day of prefishing on the lower pool of the Mississippi where we were launching at Alton. But, basically after I've seen that, I will have seen the whole area that we're allowed to fish and I can get on with something that has crept more and more into my thoughts in the

19

The BASS Masters Classic is the biggest show in fishing for the pros and the fans.

past few days. I have an elk hunt awaiting me, not to mention a little quiet time to cleanse my soul.

On that final day in Alton, I had planned to fish with Clark Heinzeman, an old goose-hunting partner who knows this river pretty well. He drove down but as we awoke, we were greeted with thunder, lightning and rain. I knew I wouldn't get much accomplished in that storm and it was lightning a great deal. So I decided to scrap my plans and go elk hunting a day early.

On Aug. 29th, I headed for Wyoming to spend a couple of weeks on the top of a mountain and let my head clear. Then I turned around and came right back for the tournament scene.

My dad pulled my boat home where it will be delivered to its buyer. While she stays at home, my wife Diane is having my new boat rigged out and will pull it to the tournament for me.

From Sept. 1st through the 14th, I spent a whole two weeks way up in the mountains near Cody, Wyoming, bow hunting for elk at 9,000 feet elevation and living out of my back pack.

It was a good time for me to unwind and kind of give myself a break between seasons. They roll us through pretty long and hard on the tournament trail and it takes its toll mentally and physically. We don't get much of a break between the Classic and our first tournament. So this elk hunting trip was my way to get away.

Although I definitely escaped during my elk trip, Diane has been home, booking sports shows for next year and sending out bimonthly reports to my sponsors. She also wrote a press release for a media kit.

The main thing was to get the new boat ready for the 1991-92 season. The plan is for her to meet me at the Super 8 Motel parking lot. I am going to be there probably on Saturday, the day before the Illinois tournament begins. I have to keep my fingers crossed and hope the boat is ready and that she is able to get there on time so I can spend a day working on my gear before this whole tournament season begins again.

I drove all night from Wyoming on Sept. 13th and arrived at the Super 8 only to find that someone has cancelled my reservations. What a pain. The Ramada only has room for me for one night. The Super 8 says they will see what they can do for me for the rest of the week. It is kind of a tense situation. We'll see what they can do for me with a room.

After a phone call, Diane now knows to meet me tomorrow at the Ramada Inn. We are going to see if we can get a room at the Super 8 and work on my tackle.

Elk hunting in the Wyoming mountains is as far removed from bass fishing as you can get.

I'm pretty tired from the long drive, but I've got a pretty refreshed mental state.

Spending that time up there hunting was rehabilitating to me, mentally. I really enjoyed it. Although I didn't get an elk, I was able to enjoy a lot of beautiful country. Just get time away from fishing for a while was wonderful. People don't realize that when you spend as much time fishing as we do — a couple hundred days a year — there is sheer enjoyment in just getting away from the fishing, discussions of fishing, interviews on fishing and that kind of thing. Don't get me wrong — I love fishing, but sometimes I need to do something different.

So, we'll see what happens tomorrow if Diane gets here and we can get our room.

It will be time to start this madness all over again.

Chapter 2

Held Hostage
By a Pair of Rivers

Illinois Bassmaster Invitational
September 18-20, 1991
Illinois and Mississippi Rivers

SEPTEMBER 14th

Diane shows up at the Ramada with the new boat. Everything looks great. She has taken care of everything — all my clothes, tackle, everything in the boat. Even remembered to get my spare trolling motor. Everything looks good. The boat looks great. They've done a great job rigging it. That is one major concern off my mind right there.

Sometimes it's not easy being the wife of a professional fisherman. We have the day to get our tackle together and get a little bit of rest. Get to spend a little bit of time together since we haven't seen each other in three weeks.

Super 8 finds a room for us, but it won't be ready for a while. So, it is 11 a.m. and we're in the parking lot waiting for the available room. It is 95 degrees and the humidity is about the same and I'm just doing my tackle and making last-minute adjustments on my boat.

Although the room isn't ready until 2 p.m., I am really relaxed. A lot more relaxed than usual. My elk hunting vacation helped. But it may be it's because it is the start of a new season. I don't really have anything to feel too tense about. The standings aren't even set yet. Everybody is at zero.

The last thing I did before going to bed at 9 p.m. was to call the lockmaster for the elevation stage of the river.

SEPTEMBER 15th

First day of practice. It was really windy today and super hot — probably close to 100 degrees. The heat index was almost up to 108. They are closing the schools down because it is so hot in St. Louis. It is 86 degrees by 9 a.m. Just unbelievable.

Today wasn't really one of those days you wanted to be a bass pro. I had a lot of problems.

I never had a bite until 2 p.m. despite fishing a lot of areas I really liked in the pre-fishing period. I ran up and locked through in to the Winfield pool, which is the upper pool. I ran a lot of the main river spots, casting a 4-inch ringworm on light line to little eddies and pockets. I also flipped a 4-inch black-and-blue Big Claw, which is a technique that I use a lot.

I also cranked some wingdams with a No. 6 shad-colored Model A Bomber. There are usually a lot of fish around them, but not today.

Without a strike at 2 p.m., I tried to go back into one of the backwater areas that I really liked. It looked like a marina boat show — I've never seen so many bass boats in all my life. They must have all practiced with the same guy that I did.

The river fish can't take that kind of boat traffic. It really muddies the water up. You just can't hardly accomplish anything practice-wise because of it. The fish aren't going to bite because they are disturbed. So I just took a look at it for future reference.

I pulled out and went to another slough that I thought would be less crowded — Prairie Slough on the Missouri side. Prairie Slough is difficult to get into. The mouth of it is a long, skinny canal that takes 20 minutes to idle through. Then, the canal hangs a left and goes back into the mainland. The water was so shallow, we used a trolling motor and a push-pole for another thirty minutes to get in.

In the rear of the slough, it drops into a small lake with 4 feet of water, which is deep for the river backwater areas. Laydown logs are everywhere — thanks to some busy beavers. There are a lot of good places for the bass to be. The water in there looked good. After all the work of getting in there, I only saw one or two other boats,

Rigging up for the Illinois practice days and looking haggard from two weeks in the woods.

which made me feel pretty good. It is about 1 1/2-mile stretch that is probably 150 yards wide.

I liked it better than anywhere I saw today. I fished the upper pool on the first day because on Sundays, the boat traffic on that lower Alton pool is horrendous. I know I made the right decision fishing the upper pool this first day of practice.

Diane caught a fish over 2 pounds. We caught another keeper and another one that would not measure in that slough. As slow as the fishing was, that was still pretty inspiring.

We left Prairie Slough at 4 p.m. to make the 15-mile run back to the ramp. A barge accident in the locks kept us sitting for a couple of hours and we rode home in the dark. I was supposed to work the tournament registration tonight (hand out some Speedo Bead samples for U.S. Tackle). As it turned out, I barely made it in time for registration to register myself for the tournament. So, the lock hold-up blew that deal for me.

Got out of registration at 9:30 p.m. and made the 24-mile drive back to the room. Got in the room at 10:00 p.m. After having a pizza delivered, I finally got to sleep at 11:00 p.m.

SEPTEMBER 16th

Second day of practice. Up at 5:00 a.m. Feeling pretty bad, thanks to only six hours of sleep. It is really hard for me to go on less than eight hours of sleep. It is thundering and lightning, so I decided to turn back in until 5:45 a.m. I needed the extra sleep and I figured daylight would be pushed back at least that long by the storm.

Today, I decided to fish the Alton pool. Being Monday, the boat traffic would be down. Things like this are the kinds of things that a lot of the guys forget to take into consideration — days the traffic will be up and days the traffic will be down.

I had ruled out pre-fishing the Illinois River. If I needed to fish it, I would fish it cold from what I learned in prefishing trip.

I target the upper Alton pool. In the first three hours of fishing, I was running and gunning the mouths of the marinas, which are located in areas that the fish spawn and spend their springtime. It just looked real good to me. It was raining pretty hard and I fished a lot of good looking water. But I only managed to catch two tiny fish. I just can't believe how tough the fishing is here. It's amazing.

I'm swapping spots with other fishermen. Everybody is fishing the same type of water. I just don't think there is enough room here for a 320-man field. The spots are so limited, they really are.

After three hours, my oil alarm on my outboard goes off to find that my oil reservoir was completely empty. I've got something stuck in my motor that is pumping my oil through about as fast as it's pumping the gasoline through. I pull out of the water at 9:15 a.m. and head for the service truck about 9 miles north.

About an hour after the service crew goes to work, I'm back in business and I fished the rest of the day without a strike. Again, I'm running main-river structure like eddies and wingdams which are about all that is available in that upper Alton pool. I just can't imagine why the fish are so lethargic. They are not biting at all. Is it the boat pressure? There are just so many fishermen and the few fish living there are being caught. I really can't figure it out. I know that Prairie Slough that I fished yesterday is looking better and better to me all the time.

My outboard is still not running right, so an hour before dark, I ran back to the Yamaha service truck and pulled the boat back out of the water. The service crew finds a clogged high-speed jet in the carburetor and after a little cleaning, the son-of-a-gun is a rocket. Finally, my boat is running right. Still haven't located very many fish, but my boat is running right.

After that, I went back to room. Stopped by Rax and got something to eat. Finally ended up in bed at 9:30 p.m. Long day. Got my boat fixed, but the fishing was still pretty tough.

SEPTEMBER 17th

I'm fishing with friend and Florida pro Bernie Schultz today.

He had flown in and didn't have a new boat yet. After meeting at 6:30 a.m. at the launch ramp, we decide to trailer back up to Winfield. I like it best of the two pools.

We went up there and spent from about 7 to 11 a.m. fishing main river-stuff. The places where these fish should be holding during this time of year — mouths of the creeks, logjams, points of the islands, tips of the wingdams — and failed to produce a single strike.

At noon we decided to pull out and fish back in the Alton pool. There is one area down by the lower dam of the Alton pool that we haven't looked at. So, we sprint down to Piasaw Creek, which is midway in the Alton pool. We put back in and run to an area called Brickyard Slough, which is where a lot of tournaments have been won. Bernie and I agree that it's probably the best-looking water in the Alton pool that we had seen. It had a lot of shoreline grass and tree-tops.

I managed to catch one nice keeper, a 14-incher, on a spinnerbait. Both of us agree that if we got stuck in this Alton pool or if we ever had a partner that wanted to come down there, this would be the area that we would choose to fish.

At the end of the day, I pulled into the parking lot of the hotel where the traditional tournament pairings meeting will be held. I did my tackle in the parking lot there. I don't even go back to my hotel room — 24 miles away.

At the meeting, I drew out in the end of the second flight with a man named Doc Gimbel. We went outside and talked for the normal song-and-dance that goes along with each first-day's partner. I told him I had one area that I felt confident in — Prairie Slough in the upper pool. The idea of going through the locks scared him. I understand his position. The locks are pretty risky. He said he had an area where he caught 11 fish yesterday. He didn't think there would be that many boats in it. He felt confident in it and since I hadn't caught a limit anywhere, I felt obliged to believe him.

He wanted to fish an area called Alton Lake, which was down by the dam — the only area that I didn't prefish a month ago. So I'm going in blind. In the back of my mind I know I'm making a mistake. You know, this is what I do for a living. I fish every day and I worked awfully area to find that one area that I really feel has the potential to be a good tournament producer. Yet I'm going to go with this guy.

Gimbel does agree to fish out of my boat. He seems like a very nice man. I've just got a bad feeling that I'm making a wrong

Taking a break to collect my thoughts.

decision heading down there. But, I've made my decision and that's what I'm going to do.

SEPTEMBER 18th

The first day of competition. Waiting to launch the boat, Doc shows me what he's been catching bass on. It makes me a little nervous when I see a guy fishing with 8-pound test line and ultralight stuff in muddy water. It doesn't jive with me. But I spooled up some 8-pound line, as he instructed me to do. He was catching his fish on a No. 7 Shad Rap around riprap in Alton Lake.

We run our 23 minutes down to Alton Lake to find that the wind is howling right on his best bank. Two-foot waves are blowing up on his best section of riprap. We are trying to cast parallel to the bank, but his lighter equipment is allowing the lure to be blown up on the bank.

It doesn't take me a whole lot of time to figure out that this water is too churned up and muddy. I immediately changed to a spinnerbait, hoping to draw a strike or two. We fished about a mile of the riprap without a strike — with boats in front and behind us. It looks like everybody and their brother has found Doc's fish. I had an uneasy feeling pretty early.

In the back of Alton Lake where there is grass lining the water, there was a boat about every 40 feet. I counted 26 boats in all in this area. By the time we got to the back where most of the fish were located, it was obvious that most of the fish had already been caught. This is not my partner's fault. It's nobody's fault. Just bad circumstances.

I have trouble fishing around a lot of boats. It's a mental thing with me. I like to be on my own. I like to be fishing water that has not been fished. I can't get into a crowd and really feel comfortable.

We stayed there until noon with just one short fish (an 11-incher that hit a 4-inch ringworm) to show for our efforts. I suggested to Doc that we needed to make a move to another area. He was more than willing and apologized for the lack of fish in his area.

So we went to Brickyard Slough — and found 10 boats waiting for us. One belongs to Woo Daves who turns out to be the leader of the day with a little over 11 pounds. As it turns out, two other anglers would catch top-10 weights from that spot the first day.

So it was obviously a pretty darn good place. I just got there too late. But hindsight is always 20-20. I wasn't in synch today.

I fished hard there until quitting time and then headed back without a single keeper. Most of the fish in the tournament were caught in both of the two areas we fished by flipping a 4-inch imitation

29

crawfish in a black and chartreuse. Or in Woo Daves case, we found later that he was fishing an 8-inch black plastic worm, which was larger than everybody else was using. That may have been the difference.

After the embarrassment of not having anything to bring to the scales, I found that I had drawn a young guy from Florida for the second day. As luck would have it, he had caught only one fish and has no water to go to. He is willing to lock through with me into the Winfield pool tomorrow and fish this Prairie Slough that I have confidence in. Maybe tomorrow is my day to get back in to the game.

Diane and I went to Ponderosa for dinner and talked a little bit about how disappointing today was. But I'm optimistic because it only takes 2 pounds, 11 ounces, to get into the money after Day One. All I need is a couple bites to get back in to it. Tomorrow is another day.

SEPTEMBER 19th

The second day of competition. Temperature is a lot cooler than it was the rest of the week. We had a front come through and the temperature dropped to 53 degrees. Its pretty darn cold compared to the 90s we've been used too. It was spitting a little rain first thing in the morning before clearing up. And it's windy, very windy.

We make our 35-minute run up the Illinois River to the Mississippi lock. There are already about 15 boats waiting on the lock. By the time the lock is open we have fished down below the locks for probably 45 minutes to an hour without a strike. We're able to enter the locks at approximately 8:05 a.m. There are 27-30 boats in the locks. Somewhere in that area. It was hard to count them all.

Once the locks open, it's like the starting flag at the Indy 500 — 30 boats wheeling out of a lock with walls on each side. It's real narrow and there are lots of waves. You have to be careful not to run into each other or the side of the walls when you're taking out of there. It's kind of a hairy deal.

Fifteen miles later, I arrive in Prairie Slough to find Ron Shuffield is right on my tail. Obviously he's fishing in there as well. He tells me if I trim my engine up high enough I can get in there without using my trolling motor. He passes me. I follow Ron and we idle in there. I look behind me and Johnnie Borden is behind me. Now there are three of us heading up into the area. I had not counted on this many people being there, but's still a big area with plenty of room.

The wind is blowing pretty hard. I begin my day by flipping a 4-inch plastic crawfish with an 1/8-ounce sinker on 20-pound test line. The water is 2 feet where I'm flipping a lot of laydowns. I'm going to fish it real slow because by now the sun is out and it's bright and shiny. It's also very cold. I know this cold front is going to make the fish hold tight to the cover.

After 45 minutes without a strike, I noticed a shad come out of the water near the base of a log. I dropped my flipping stick and grabbed another rod with the 3/8-ounce spinnerbait. I fired it past that log and slowly rolled it across the wood where my first keeper bass of the tournament nailed it. It turned out to be a 3-pound, 4-ounce largemouth — and a pretty good hint to drop the flipping stick and keep throwing the spinnerbait. That's a pretty good fish in this pool as tough as the tournament is. I was back in the hunt.

Tournament Tip

An important lesson that any angler can learn from occurred when I spotted my biggest bass chasing shad. I immediately changed baits to one that was more applicable for the situation — a lure that imitated a shad. That bass was chasing shad near the top of deep brush, so I switched to a spinnerbait, which is a better choice as a shad-imitator. The lesson here is to be aware of any changes or activity around you and don't be afraid to change baits in mid-stream — even for one cast.

I made about another 30 to 40 casts with the spinnerbait and I caught a 1 1/4-pound bass. Now I'm in pretty good shape. Things look real good and I'm really motivated. I've got maybe about 4 1/2 pounds in the livewell and it's early. If I can get one more 2- to 3-pound fish, I'm going to make a paycheck in one day. And who knows what tomorrow would bring.

I fished without another strike until 12:30 p.m. Ron Shuffield and Johnnie Borden came out of the slough, saying they hadn't had a strike.

I allowed myself 2 1/2 hours to get back to the launch ramp —enough time to get out of the slough, down to the locks and through. At 1:30 p.m., I made the move. With a respectable 4 1/2 pounds in the livewell, I headed for the locks.

As I approached the locks, I noticed a barge coming towards me in the locks and that the locks were up. This usually means he is going to pull right out and I can pull right in and go through. But I also noticed there were no other tournament boats in the area which kind of made me a little uneasy.

I fished around for probably 20 minutes and the barge never came out. Well, another 20 minutes went by and before the lockmaster comes out and says it's going to be at least an hour and a half before he can get me through. I tell you, it's probably one of the coldest feelings I have ever had come over me. I knew then that I was going to be late for weigh in. I've got 4 1/2 pounds of fish in the box. I'm helpless.

I told the lockmaster he had to do something. He had to get me through. I have a good bag of fish. There's got to be some way that you can get me through the lock. He said he couldn't. That it was a double lock barge. I asked him if he could lock me between the two sets of barges. He refused, saying it was against procedure.

So I sat there and waited — even fished around a little bit. I thought I could pester him in to letting me through. But it never happened. I waited almost an hour and a half before the locks finally opened and I was allowed to go in with several other of the boats who were also late. The difference was that none of them had a fish.

When the lock doors opened, I had 17 minutes to get to the ramp. It's about a 30-minute run. I cut every corner and ran as hard as I could, but I was still nine minutes late, which scratched my day's catch. I weighed my catch in anyway. I worked hard for those fish. Although my 4 1/2 pounds of fish was disqualified, it would have been enough to put me in the money.

Needless to say, it was a very disappointing day. The only way it could have been any worse is if that 4 1/2 pounds would have belonged to my partner and I would have been the one to decide to keep us up there until we were late. At least it was my call, my fish, my loss.

It's still a good area. I've seen a couple good fish come out of there now. I'm going to go back there tomorrow and maybe catch 6 to 7 pounds. It looks like cashing a check is going to take about 6 pounds.

My partner for tomorrow is Bucky Bonner, a fellow Skeeter team member from Texas, who hasn't caught a fish in two days. He is more than willing to go back with me up to Prairie Slough.

Me, Diane, California pro Bryon Velvick and a friend, Doug Shaiper, went out to dinner and talked about the day's events. It was good to unwind a bit. I was in bed by 9:30 p.m.

SEPTEMBER 20th

The final day of competition. Up at 4:45 a.m. Diane is going to go with me to bring the truck back so she can pack up all of our gear and meet me at the ramp after the tournament. Then we can head for home.

Meeting Bucky at the take-off at 6 a.m., it's very cold this morning. The temperature is in the upper 30s and there is a little bit of frost on things actually. It's probably going to be the toughest fishing day of the three. (as if we need it any tougher). Today is the day I need a big catch.

Winning Ways

For three blustery days, Woo Daves proved he may be the best river fisherman in America, scratching out 11 bass weighing 18 pounds, 11 ounces. His winning lure was an 8-inch Texas-rigged Mister Twister Phenom worm with a 3/16-ounce bullet weight on 15- and 20-pound test line. His fish were caught from a highly pressured slough area off of the Mississippi River. He fished sparse grass patches in shallow water, pitching worms along the edge and working them slowly back to the boat. Most of the strikes occurred along the edge of the vegetation.

Bucky only brings a couple of rods. A spinnerbait rod and a flipping stick. We are first flight so we are limited on the amount of time we'll have to fish. Another strike against us.

Waiting for the locks to open, we fished around for about 30 minutes. We get through the locks a little bit quicker than yesterday and I noticed there are about as many boats locking up as there were the day before. One of the boats I don't see is Ron Shuffield's who was in Prairie Slough the day before. So, hopefully, I'll have a little bit less competition.

We're actually fishing by 8:05 a.m., which is a really good thing. We start off by flipping. It's very calm, bright and sunny. Very conducive to flipping. I start off with a 3/8-ounce Weapon Jig on 20-pound test line. Bucky is flipping a straight Big Claw, which is also black and chartreuse. That seems to be a very good color in muddy or light to moderately stained water, which is what we were fishing. Both of us using very light weights because of the shallow water and the slow fall that we were looking for.

We methodically worked our way along the bank. After about one hour without a strike, we were fishing a very large tree with a lot of places for a bass to be. Bucky sets a hook on the first bite and catches a nice fish — about a 3 1/2-pounder. He struggled quite a bit to get the fish out of the tree. I used the trolling motor to take him into the tree where he could get it out and into the boat. He was pretty happy. It is the first fish for him in the tournament. That gave us a little momentum.

We fished hard for four more hours without a bite, alternating the spinnerbait and jig according to the cover. With about 20 minutes left to fish before leaving, I flipped my jig into an overhanging bush and it had only sunk about an inch when a nice fish came up and took it off the surface. I dropped my rod tip and set the hook and quickly swung a 2-pound, 2-ounce bass in to the boat. Immediately it occurred to me that I probably would have been in the money with that fish had I not had the lock problem the day before. Everybody was predicting 6 pounds to make the money. This fish would have given me close to 6 1/2 pounds.

Fighting off such thoughts, I fished until 12:30 without another bite. Bucky and I left with one fish apiece. After arriving at the locks, they quickly locked every one through.

After fishing main-river stuff for the last hour of the day, I proceeded to the weigh-in to find a huge, enthusiastic crowd. I signed lots of autographs. It was just great.

While securing my boat for the trip home, I had to stop and sign a lot of autographs, which was very tough in a way. It's so easy when you have a bad tournament to just walk away and get in your truck. In reality, what you have to do is grin and bear it and go back in and be a part of the crowd. They are here to see us, the pro fishermen. We have to make sure we don't snub them just because we had a bad tournament. That's the worst thing we could do.

So Diane and I spent some time with the spectators and watched Woo Daves get his victory plaque. I was really glad for him.

We drove most of the evening from about 7:00 to midnight. I'm really tired and very irritable. Just trying to focus on getting home. We know that we're only going to have about 24 hours at the house because we have to leave for a Golden Blend tournament the day after tomorrow. It will not be the glamorous side of professional fishing, either. We'll spend most of the day working on the boat, doing laundry and packing back up for the next trip.

Chapter 3

Bass Fishing's Lucrative Cast

B.A.S.S. MegaBucks Tournament
October 7-12, 1991
Chickamauga and Nickajack Lakes

OCTOBER 4th

Got up this morning at about 7:00 a.m. Loaded the van and headed for Chattanooga, Tenn., for the MegaBucks Tournament.

On the way I stopped just north of the city and visited a friend that lives on Watt's Bar. Talked to him a little bit about what had been going on there — a little bit about the Chickamauga water level and temperature and how their success had been the last month or so. According to him, the upper end of the lake still has plenty of milfoil. So the spinnerbait, buzzbait and rat or Snagproof frog will be hot baits. Also, flipping a jig or a crawfish should work pretty well. I bought a few baits that I thought we might need down here.

We finally got to the Red Roof Inn just east of the lake at about 5:00 p.m. this evening. I spent about an hour and a half doing my tackle. A front is starting to come in. It looks like it's going to be cold throughout the weekend (the practice period) and then clear off and get even colder the first competition days of the tournament.

With that in mind, I want to try to establish a deep pattern if possible so I tied on a couple of large crankbaits and a Carolina-rigged lizard for fishing the edge of the river channel and some deep ledges.

The next 30 minutes were spent going over my map and just finalizing things. MegaBucks is the most lucrative tournament on the B.A.S.S. trail with a $100,000 payday, so I want to get a good jump and get two full days of practice in before the competition begins.

I plan to trailer up the Tennessee River to the mouth of the Hiawassee River. I'll fish the upper two-thirds of Chickamauga tomorrow, probably. I expect the tournament to be won there because that's where the majority of the grass is located at this time. Most of the grass at the lower end of the lake has been killed and I think that the fish, with the water cooling down to the mid-70s, will definitely begin to move shallow. The grass and laydown wood are obvious places for them to be.

My confidence is pretty high after talking to everybody. The Bass' n' Gal Tournament began today here and Chris Houston is leading with only 8 pounds. Five fish that weigh 8 pounds. Large catches are not the rule, but it's got to be better than Alton, Ill.

OCTOBER 5th

First day of practice. Up at 5:00 a.m. Left the room at 5:30 a.m. Headed for the north end of the lake. Decided to put in at the ferry crossing on the upper section of the river.

As daylight arrives, it is cloudy and overcast and kind of balmy. Perfect topwater and spinnerbait conditions.

Diane and I both fished a buzzbait and spinnerbait quite a bit in the backwater sloughs. Diane caught one about 3 pounds on a scattered grassline back in a slough. But after several hours of fishing sloughs, we were having trouble getting any bites. It looks like because the water temperature is dropping, the fish have pulled out to the main river channel.

I decided it would be better to concentrate our efforts on the main river grassline where the bass have easy access to deep water. We managed to catch several keepers and one about 3 1/4 pounds on the main river grasslines. I tried to concentrate on areas that had a well-defined edge to the grass adjacent to deep water. With a cold front coming, these bass should stop hitting a buzzbait and spinnerbait. But they will re-position themselves on the edge of the grass, where I can probably catch them flipping when the sun comes out.

It turned out to be a pretty good day for fishing. It got cold by the afternoon. We fished from daylight until dark, putting in a 12-hour day. Came in and hooked the charger up. After tournament registration, working on tackle and a delivered pizza, we got in bed at 8:45 p.m.

OCTOBER 6th

Second day of practice. The day awoke very cold, windy and clear. Diane decided to stay in so I practiced on my own. She launched me at the lower end of the lake down around Harrison Bay State Park.

I planned on fishing main river ledges today — cranking a large crankbait along the main river drops (particularly drops that have a creek channel that feeds into the main river). This main river ledge is about 6 feet and drops off to about 25 feet. It's a good place for fish to live.

I went out and attempted to fish that pattern for several hours but because of the wind, I was unable to stay out there very long. It really hampered my practice. Very cold, windy conditions.

I went to a large bay in the very back of Soddy Creek, where I've caught a lot in grass bass in the past. But that's the past. They've killed every bit of grass on the lower end of Chickamauga Lake. It never ceases to amaze me. They have such a great thing here and then they go and kill all of the grass making the fishing tough. They talk about how they want this to become the fishing capital of the world and then they kill the number one thing that keeps the fishermen coming — the fish habitat. It just amazes me.

The only thing back there for the fish to relate to is the riprap. I caught two small keepers by jerking a chrome-and-blue Rogue. With the bright sun and clear water, I thought a Rogue would be a good bet. I caught five or six non-keepers and two that were barely keepers.

I realized that the main lake is where I needed to be but the wind was so intense that fishing deep water structure of any kind was almost out of the question. So I moved to the bank, fishing chunk rock and alternating with bluff rock — just trying to find out if the fish are on any specific type of rock. I caught several more small fish and a couple of keepers just casting a spinnerbait past downed trees and along the rocky banks.

I learned very little today. It was very discouraging. I don't know what the front is going to do to the upper river grass beds, but it looks like that's my best bet. I wish I could have established a deep pattern, but it just didn't happen. I don't feel very confident, but a lot of the fishermen are talking like they are having trouble catching them. This front has really put the "slammy whammy" on the fish.

After a quick bite to eat, I arrived at the tournament briefing. I drew veteran Texas pro Randy Fite, who thinks that he has a couple areas where he can catch a limit of fish by jigging a 1-ounce jigging spoon in 16 to 18 feet of water. He's looking for shad on his graph and staying on top of them with the flasher unit and dropping a spoon on them. The fish are right on the bottom and this is a pretty good way of catching them this time of the year. He also says he's catching a few on a Carolina rig.

In the morning, we'll fish Randy's areas and once the sun gets up, then we'll run to my grass beds. The only problem is that there is about a 40-minute run between my area and his spots. I've decided to ride with Randy tomorrow because the use of his electronics on this area with the graph is very important and I wouldn't want to hamper him. With my pattern, I'll be primarily flipping the edges of grasslines so the use of my Skeeter boat wouldn't be that important. He has a foot-controlled trolling motor which is my only criteria for whether I use his boat or mine.

OCTOBER 7th

First competition day. I met Randy at 6:15 a.m. — our flight is due to go out at 7:30. We put in at Harrison Bay and drove across the lake in the fog to Dallas Bay. The fog was so thick we couldn't see 50 feet in front of the boat. We had to idle quite a bit before we could run. It is very, very cold, with frost in the boat this morning — one of the coldest mornings of the year so far.

After a short run, we stop at Randy's first spot, a sloping point that breaks off into 25 feet of water. It has very little cover or structure on the bottom. I would have never stopped and fished there. The only reason he's here is because the shad are on this break and the bass are underneath them.

I caught the first three fish of the day on a 1-ounce jigging spoon, jigging it vertically off the bottom, snapping it and letting it fall. Randy caught twice as many fish as I did, but I managed to catch the first three keepers. All were very small keeper fish.

Throughout the morning, we rotated between two or three areas. All were within sight of each other. Randy got an occasional bite, but I didn't get another strike. He ended up catching the next four. I didn't get another bite until 11 a.m. Randy completed his limit by 1 p.m. by just alternating from area to area. I caught quite a few under-sized fish in the afternoon, but couldn't manage another keeper.

I noticed some shad scattering and blowing up in a pocket near where we were spooning. I suggested to Randy that maybe we should ease up in that pocket and throw a spinnerbait to these fish that were active in the shallower water. One of my first casts with a spinnerbait produced a keeper. That was my fifth and final fish of the day. Randy ended up culling one fish on a jigging spoon. His limit (seven bass) weighed 6 pounds, 2 ounces. My five bass weighed a measly 4 pounds, 2 ounces.

The first day — one of the coldest of the year

But both catches were fairly respectable considering that very few heavy-weight stringers were brought in. Larry Nixon is leading with just over 10 pounds.

I'm fishing with Randy Romig tomorrow. Randy caught a good limit today — around 7 pounds. He's in the top 20. I'm obliged to ride with him and fish his areas early.

I didn't get a chance to go to my areas today. I felt that staying down there and catching a limit would be a good day, considering how tough the conditions were (bright, clear and cold). Tomorrow will be the third day after the cold front. I believe that the grass bass will become a little more active. I'm going to fish Randy's areas in the morning and run to mine in the afternoon.

I'm pretty edgy tonight. Lately I have left a lot of control of my destiny to my partners. It really bothers me — not getting to use my boat, not getting to fish the type of water and the areas that I am best suited to fish. It makes me feel kind of out of control. Therefor, I feel pretty edgy and apprehensive about the day.

I really need to make the top 50 cut, which comes after Wednesday. But my goal is to return to the finals (like I did in finishing sixth last year), where the top 10 finishers fish for the big money — $100,000. It's important financially and to my Classic weight. The first three days' weight of MegaBucks can be used as a wild card toward the Classic at the end of the year.

And this is no small financial investment, either. The entry fee is $2,000.

OCTOBER 8th

Second day of competition. Met my partner, Randy Romig at Harrison Bay. We rode across the lake to Dallas Bay where the tournament was to take off. Very cold. Frost on the boats this morning. Crystal clear blue sky. Obviously tough high pressure fishing conditions.

Randy had been catching most of his fish on a Carolina-rigged worm (3/4-ounce sinker, 2-foot leader and 12-pound test line). My Carolina rig also includes a Speedo Bead. I was using a 4-inch smoke silver flake Kalin grub. The key areas seemed to be large bays or coves off the main lake that had a lot of shad in them.

Basically, we're fishing the same type of pattern that Randy Fite and I had fished the day before only with a different lure. Our strategy was to follow the shad with our electronics and cast to them with a Carolina rig. The day before, Romig had caught an easy limit doing this in two bays near the main lake. But it was much tougher today. In three hours on his best area, I caught one bass. He had caught none. The baitfish were suspended off the bottom. They were stratified a little bit higher in the water making it much more difficult to catch the bass. I realize that hindsight is 20-20, but we might have been better off cranking through them with a shallow running crankbait.

We moved to his second area at approximately 10:30 a.m. I caught my second keeper bass of the day. Randy proceeded to catch two keepers in the same area. We fished the area until 12:30 p.m. At this time I felt strongly that with the sun warming the water, my grassy areas in the north end of the lake would become warmed up and the fishing would be better up there. Since his fish weren't biting, I suggested running to my area. He agreed so I drove his boat up to my best grass area.

There was some movement. There were shad in the grass. It was a promising situation. I alternated between fishing a Snagproof frog across the matted grass and flipping the edges with a black-and-blue jig.

My strategy did not work. We were short on time because it was a 45-minute run to the area north of the Hiawassee River. We caught one undersized bass the entire afternoon.

It was a very discouraging day. Nothing my partners have done or I've done seems to work. But we weren't alone in our frustration. Most anglers brought in one or two fish and the most successful caught five or six small bass.

I have approximately 6 pounds after two days. I'm 2 pounds, 11 ounces out of the money and it looks like it will take 12 pounds to get a check. I've drawn a partner that will do whatever I want tomorrow. I know there have been several big fish caught cranking deep ledges with big crankbaits. I have a couple of confidence areas where feeder creeks intersect the main river channel, so that's my game plan for tomorrow. I know if I can get two bites doing that, I can get the 6 or 7 pounds I need to make the cut.

Tournament Tip

Cover like aquatic vegetation, stumps and laydown trees are not the only criteria for bass to hold in an area. Large concentrations of baitfish can also keep bass in an area for long periods of time, particularly in the fall. Anglers should keep this in mind and fish under or through the baitfish to catch these active bass. Crankbaits and jigging spoons are excellent choices for situations like this.

OCTOBER 9th

Third day of competition and the cut to the top 50. Up at 5:30. Hook my boat up. First day I get to use my boat this week. I drove to Dallas Bay. Fog was extremely thick. I didn't want to put in and try to run across the lake. A lot of the anglers did. I drove to Dallas Bay and met my partner. We dropped in the water about 7:15. Check out time is 7:30 a.m., but the fog keeps the tournament field waiting until 9:30. I really needed the long day to catch up and I'm in an early flight. But now I've got a very short day because of the two-hour fog delay.

When they turned us loose from Dallas Bay, the visibility was moderate. But by the time we hit the main river channel, visibility was less then 30 yards. Boats were flying every where. It was a very dangerous situation. I obviously was not going to sit out on the main river ledge with boats flying all around me. I decided to pull into a cove and just fish. It's very discouraging. I could feel the clock ticking away.

I threw a little crankbait in a shallow cove. I had no idea where I was even fishing, but it was probably a mile from the takeoff. I did manage to catch five undersized bass.

We fished there until 10:30 a.m. when the fog finally lifted enough to where I could see where I was going. I proceeded north to the Sale Creek area of Lake Chickamauga and began cranking feeder creeks that fed in to the main river channel with a deep-diving Tennessee shad-patterned crankbait on 12-pound Stren line.

I concentrated on fishing the junction points formed by the intersection of the creek and main river. The idea was to bounce the crankbait off the stumps and the lip of the old river channel. I was keeping my boat in about 14 feet of water and fishing the 6-foot ledge. Again, I knew I wouldn't get many bites but two bites off of this spot could weigh 7 to 10 pounds. There are always big fish out there this time of the year. I made it work in the Golden Blend Championship last year. Here at the same time of the year, I was going to try to make it work again.

After two hours, I hadn't had a strike on the main river channel. At about 1 p.m., the marker buoys on the main river channel indicated that there was water being generated. With that in mind, I immediately thought of the main river laydown trees further up the lake, where the bass should be active. This is another pattern for catching one or two big bass. And that's what I needed — a couple of big bites. Time was not on my side at this point.

After running up river, I began flipping the main river channel trees without any success for an hour and a half. Finally, I caught a 1 1/2-pound bass, which turned out to be my only fish of the day. I fished the main river channel trees until it was time to come in. My check in was 3:40. So, I had a very short day. By the time the fog burned off, it was 10:30 and I had to start back in at 3:00. It left me very little time.

I ended up with a total weight of 7 pounds, 8 ounces. This will be my wild card tournament, erasing the 2 pounds, 2 ounces from Alton, Ill. That might not seem like much, but that 5 or 6 pounds could make the difference in whether I qualify for the Classic or not. I have to think positive.

It took 11 pounds, 10 ounces to make the top 50 cut. Most of the fishermen who did well had been in coves where high concentrations of shad were and using little chrome crankbaits on fairly light line (cranking it through the shad in the middle of the coves). They were not fishing around any type of cover. This is one pattern that I did not expand upon in practice. I guess I misjudged how much weight it would take to make the cut. I didn't have any idea that 4 pounds a day would put me in the money in this tournament.

With MegaBucks over for me, there is no reason to hang around. After dropping the boat at the hotel, we went to dinner with

Rich Tauber, who is staying next to us. He missed the cut as well. We went to an Italian restaurant, ate and talked about the tournament a little bit. A movie got my mind off of the tournament for a little while. Diane and I finally got to bed about 10 p.m.

We'll stay in Chattanooga a couple more days. Tomorrow will be spent re-organizing everything, packing and running errands. The next day, I'm scheduled to take two outdoor writers fishing while the 10 finalists fish for the big MegaBucks money.

Winning Ways

Larry Nixon owns the MegaBucks event. This was his fourth MegaBucks victory. In the preliminary rounds, Nixon targeted rocks in Chickamauga in areas where the vegetation has disappeared. The most productive rocks were adjacent to deep water and had shad activity. Rocks paid off in the finals for Nixon, who used a 3/8-ounce Stanley Vibra-Shaft spinnerbait with a No. 3 gold willowleaf blade in front of a No. 4 Colorado blade. A tiny 1/8-ounce white Bomber Mini-Whacker spinnerbait produced on pressured bass in the final round. The key to winning the MegaBucks format is "fishing everything that's in your hole very efficiently and not missing any fish or leaving any for anybody else," Nixon believes.

Friday afternoon, we're off to Columbia, S.C., site of the Bassmaster Top 100 on Lake Murray and a chance for quick redemption.

43

South Carolina's Lake Murray has become one of America's greatest bass lakes.

Chapter 4

A Chance
For Quick Redemption

South Carolina BASSMASTER Top 100
October 16-19, 1992
Lake Murray

OCTOBER 11th

I gave a call to a friend of mine, Mike Doss, who lives here in Columbia. He came over to the house we're renting right on Lake Murray. While he was there, we went over the map a little bit and discussed patterns.

From what he was saying, the most effective patterns have been slow-rolling spinnerbaits through deep elodeagrass or fishing floating worms over the shallow bars and stumpy points. Another pattern would be flipping a jig or throwing a spinnerbait up the river.

OCTOBER 12th

Today was spent getting my tackle ready. Other than that, I bought a fishing license and drove around to familiarize myself with the area. That was pretty much all that we did today. Got in bed fairly early — about 8:30 p.m.

OCTOBER 13th

First day of practice. Launching near the dam, my intentions for today were to basically fish shallow with topwater baits in the morning and then move in to the deeper elodea grass as the day progressed. But the wind really hampered my deep grass fishing and made it difficult to stay out in the main lake.

Diane caught a 5-pound bass early on a spinnerbait. The fish had shown interest in my Zara Spook and she followed with a spinnerbait. Then it was several hours before we had another bite. I fished a lot of the deep grass with a spinnerbait and Carolina-rigged lizard without any success. The wind finally became so unbearable on the open water that I resorted to fishing secondary points in the mouths of coves with a white floating worm that's so popular here. The worm is rigged on a 4/0 hook, 14-pound test line with a little swivel in the front of it and about a 14-inch leader. The swivel helps weigh the bait and get it down.

The floating worm on these wind-blown points produced two nice fish. I was concentrating on areas where the water was deep but came up to a very shallow, flat shoal. I ran that kind of pattern the rest of the day and had a few other bites, but I shook them off. But not nearly as many strikes as I had expected.

Tomorrow I plan to go up the river and fish shallow. I'll flip most of the day. I'm going to throw topwater baits down in the lower lake where the water is clear early and then about 9:30 a.m. or so make a change — run up the lake and fish a spinnerbait or a jig in the blowdowns and around docks. Hopefully with more success than I had today.

Diane fixed a great Mexican dinner tonight. It's nice to have a house instead of a hotel room where she can cook dinner every night. You really appreciate some conveniences — not to mention the time saved — when you come in tired off of the water.

OCTOBER 14th

Second day of practice. I'm on the water as soon as it was light enough to navigate safely. I was trying to take advantage of the low-light situation, trying to fish as many shallow, flat, clear-water points as I could in the morning with a Zara Spook and a Pop-R. It looks like another high, clear day.

Diane caught two keepers on a spinnerbait before I had my first bite on the Zara Spook. My first bite, however, was a 5-pounder. That's two 5-pounders in two days on a Zara Spook early in the morning.

I stayed with the Spook until about 9:30 a.m. and never had another bite on it. Then I headed up river and began alternating between boat docks, blowdowns and any other visible cover in Little Saluda, a branch of the main river that feeds Lake Murray. I was fishing a 1/2-ounce brown jig-and-pork frog along with a 3/8-ounce chartreuse-and-white spinnerbait with a single Colorado blade.

Up the river, I hit a stretch of docks that had brushpiles on them. In about 45 minutes, I had three bites, which I shook off. One of those fish weighed about 6 or 7 pounds and came completely out of the bush to eat my jig. I let her swim with it until she pulled free. But I know where that one lives.

Changing areas slightly, we fished a nearby pocket or two. Diane caught a 2 1/2-pounder and another keeper. I had two keepers on a spinnerbait after that. The area seems to have had quite a few fish in it. I proceeded on up the little Saluda to the very head waters, but the further up I went, the worse the fishing seemed to get and the clearer the water got.

That area just above the split of the two rivers seems to be the best. It also has the dirtiest water that I was able to find. At least I have one confidence area. If it stays sunny, that would be a good pattern.

I arrived home at dark, in time for Diane's lasagne that she had in the refrigerator from the day before. After that, it was time to go through the usual tournament registration routine, so I rode into town with Randy Moseley. It's 9:00 and I'm going to bed.

OCTOBER 15th

Last day of practice. Today was a pretty eventful day. I had intended to fish the grass today, but the weather didn't cooperate. The wind blew hard, eliminating any chances to fish open water. I looked for sheltered water in the morning and threw a Pop-R and Zara Spook trying to locate another big bass or two for the competition days.

I looked for calm water where I could expand on that Zara Spook pattern. But I only managed to catch a small keeper today on it. I stayed with it until about 9:30 a.m., then the sun got pretty bright. It was a clear crisp day.

I decided to make a run north to the Big Saluda River. I had fished the Little Saluda River yesterday. With the wind killing my grass pattern, the Big Saluda seems like the only sheltered alternative when looking at new water.

It was cloudy and starting to rain when I stopped on the first bank. My first or second cast with a spinnerbait to the shallow shoreline grass between a couple of boat docks produced a bass a little over 7 pounds. About 20 feet farther down the bank, I caught a 3-pounder. I had seen enough of this area, so we left immediately.

Being located near the main river channel seems to be the key to each of the productive areas. I can't catch them in the backs of the creeks or coves. The bass are relating to main lake or main river channel structure — whether it be docks or laydowns or what have you.

Overall, it was a good day of practice, especially when you consider that my primary pattern had been wiped out by the wind. I could have had a 20-pound stringer today with the 7-pound kicker. I feel pretty good about it.

We've got some cloud cover starting to move in. They are predicting a low pressure system blowing through. It should make the fishing pretty good tomorrow. I'm very optimistic.

With the Top 100 pro-am format, I'm fishing with an amateur so I control my water — for the first time this season. My game plan is to try and catch a fish or two down in the lower end of the lake in the clear water on topwater baits and then run up the river and fish as much of the good water as I can, particularly boat docks and blowdowns and brushpiles around the docks.

The partner pairings meeting tonight was a long, drawn out affair. I met my amateur partner for tomorrow. Lonnie Stanley had some spinnerbaits for me. When it was over, Moseley and I headed back and did our tackle. We were in bed by 10:00. Later night then we had planned.

OCTOBER 16th

First day of competition. One of the most disappointing days of my fishing career, and I mean that. I'm very, very disheartened about my performance today.

I only weighed in one bass (weighing a pound and an ounce). It's really not typical for me to do as well in practice and fish as poorly in the tournament as I did this first day.

My day began with a howling north west wind which was blowing into most of my good topwater areas. Calm water was difficult, actually impossibe, to find. So the topwater pattern was out. I tried to make it work for about two hours, but I just couldn't manage to get a bite on a Zara Spook.

I proceeded up the river. The day was a mixture of clouds and sunshine. It would rain a little bit and then the sun would come out. It was a very erratic day. I was unable to catch them on my boat docks flipping a jig. I don't think the sun was bright enough. And it looked like they had pulled about 6 more inches of water out of the lake, which made my shallow docks even shallower.

A jig flipped into a log produced this keeper.

It was like I was a step behind all day. Every pocket I'd pull into had a boat in it or there was a boat just leaving. It was like I was out of synch all day. It's a really sick feeling. You fish with a knot in your stomach all day.

The day finished in perfect form. Fishless with about 20 minutes remaining, I hooked a giant bass. I flipped a jig into some shoreline grass next to a dock when I felt the strike. I set the hook immediately. I really didn't realize how large it was until it came to the surface. When it headed back down, I should have bowed to her to release a little pressure. Instead I tried to lean on her a little too hard and I broke my 20-pound test line.

Obviously, a tough, tough day. That was one of the most disappointing things that could ever happen. I managed to catch my one 1-pound, 1-ounce fish 10 minutes before I came in on a floating worm on a wind-blown point.

Tonight Diane and I went to a nearby Baptist church. A fellow pro, Alton Jones, was going to share his testimony. It's always good for me, especially when things are tough, to be able to listen to The Word and be able to escape from fishing for a little while. It kept us out a little later then we like, but we enjoyed it. By the time I had my tackle done, it was almost 10 p.m. again.

OCTOBER 17th

Second day of competition. I started the day knowing that I have a lot of ground to make up, based on yesterday's big catches.

I really feel that the only way I can catch up in this tournament is with a Zara Spook. So I stayed with the Spook for nearly three hours this morning. The wind was not as intense, so I was able to fish a few more areas.

I managed to catch two bass early on the Spook. I fished it until 10 a.m. without much success. My amateur partner who knew the lake very well, took me to several areas with good brush-filled docks that had a little deeper water on them. I fished those quite thoroughly for three hours and never had a bite.

I've really resigned myself to the fact now that they are not on those brushy docks anymore. The water has just gotten too low.

The rest of my day, I fished wind-blown points with a floating worm. I only hooked one fish all afternoon — a 3-pounder that escaped in a brushpile. It has not been a very efficient tournament so far for me. I'm not getting very many bites and then I'm not capitalizing on the bites that I'm getting. That makes it even worse.

That's pretty much it . I really don't know what most of the guys are doing. I'm rooming with Randy Moseley, who is in fifth place. He's catching some fish on topwater in the morning and he's running way up the river to crank chunk rock banks late in the day. There is very little of that kind of bank up there. I want to stay out of his way. I don't want to cause him any problems, yet I've got to try and catch some, too. I'll take that little bit of knowledge and try and work with it.

Diane and I had to keep a couple of fish from weigh-in to use for pictures for one of my sponsors, Snagproof Lures, for advertisement purposes.

Diane fixed a real nice dinner here at the house and we just sat around and relaxed for a few minutes. First time I've had a chance to do that. I'm feeling very discouraged. I don't really know which direction I should be heading tomorrow. I plan on fishing topwater early again and probably proceeding up the river and trying to make something happen. That's about it. It's 8:30 p.m., and I'm going to get in bed early tonight.

OCTOBER 18th

Third day of competition. Starting off in the second leg of the third flight, I missed a little bit of the topwater time this morning. Every few minutes of low-light conditions is critical. The sun has been bright and shinny. I can't hardly get a bite on the topwater past 8:30 a.m.

After two hours without a strike, I decide to make the run up the river and fish laydowns and docks and work my way up the Little

Saluda River. Basically, I'm going to fish up as far as I can — try and get away from other people and find some water that hasn't been fished so much. There are a lot of laydowns up there in the Little Saluda River.

My run was interrupted when my outboard began vibrating violently. Trimming the motor up, I saw that one of the prop blades was

missing. With my partner holding me by my feet, I hung over the lower unit and changed props. That ordeal cost me 45 valuable minutes.

I stopped on a row of docks where I had shaken a 5- or 6-pound fish earlier in the week during practice. I tried her the first day of the tournament, tried her again today and still no go. I fished the whole line of docks hoping that maybe a new fish had moved up or that fish had relocated. I wasn't able to get a strike.

I was flipping a 1/2 ounce pumpkinseed Weapon Jig with a Kalin Salty Craw pumpkin-pepper trailer. The water has cleared up quite a bit and that pumpkin-pepper always seems to work best in clear water (better than the standard brown jig-and-pork). It's a little bit more ghosty looking in the water. It kind of fades in. You don't see it quite as well.

Without a bite at 10:30 a.m., I began running pockets with laydown timber. The second pocket I pulled into had four blowdowns on the bank. I got a strike on the second blowdown and set the hook, but missed the fish. I threw the bait right back in and it ate it. It weighed between 3 1/4 and 3 1/2 pounds. A small keeper came off of the next tree.

I fished my way several miles up above the last bridge in the Little Saluda River. I flipped almost every log and laydown for two hours and finally had another strike. It was a bass of about 5 pounds. It pulled loose from the jig as I swung it in the boat. I was lucky I didn't lose it.

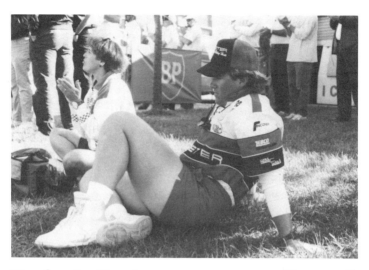

The frustration from my poor execution really shows in this picture.

That gave me a little momentum. Things were starting to happen. If I could just get a couple more bites like that I'd be back in the ball game. However, after two more hours I hadn't had a strike. I did have my fourth strike of the day at about 1:15 p.m. I set the hook on the fish, but it escaped as I swung it toward the boat. It was about a 3-pounder.

My execution in this tournament has been pathetic. I lost an 8-pounder the first day, one about 3 pounds yesterday and another 3-pounder today. I've lost as many fish in this tournament as I've caught. It's pretty sad. Very sad.

Randy Moseley, my roommate, is leading the tournament — fishing the same pattern I am. He's just making it happen. He's not missing any fish and he's getting plenty of bites. I can't understand it. I'm beside myself, but I'm very happy for him. I think he's going to win this one. I've really got a feeling about it. I hope he does. No one needs it more than he does.

Tomorrow I've drawn an amateur who is well up in the standings. He made it pretty clear to me that he wanted some water to fish. That kind of concerns me a little bit. I'll do everything I can to help him catch some fish. Hopefully, I can catch a good stringer, too.

I won't be able to make the money. I've only got 15 pounds after three days. The money is somewhere probably around 31 to 32 pounds. My chances of making the money are slim to none. But, I need to catch some weight for the Classic standings. I'll do my best.

As we pulled out of the marina tonight, we had a little problem. Diane had backed the van into a spectator's car. Now, we're heading over to meet with that man and find out how much damage was done to his car. Then we'll meet with Tim Tucker to discuss this book.

After dinner with Tim at 7 p.m. at the Comfort Inn in Lexington and a gas stop I can finally get some sleep.

OCTOBER 19th

The final day of competition. Boy, it just seems like one disappointment after another. I can't remember having so many tournaments in a row where I just couldn't make anything work.

As we were idling out, the B.A.S.S. staff member always asks you what time you're due in. The regular guy was missing and his replacement told me I was due back at 4:40 p.m. I was under the impression that my time was 4:30, but he insisted that it was 4:40 p.m. I bought it. The rules read that you have to be sure yourself. You can't listen to what anybody tells you. Even the B.A.S.S. staff. And your daily check-in time is posted.

I fished topwater baits for about two hours this morning. I did not have one strike. I proceeded all the way up the Little Saluda River. When I got in to Little Saluda River, I began flipping a 1/2-ounce jig and caught one about 2 pounds early.

About an hour later, I hooked another one about 2 1/2 pounds inside of a brushpile. I got my hand all the way down to where I could touch it, but I couldn't get my hand in his mouth. Finally, as I was ready to get my hand in his mouth, the jig pulled free and I lost him. I just ended up wet. No fish, just soaking wet.

I fished up there until about 1 p.m. without another strike. Then I moved back down river a little ways and began fishing more boat docks, figuring the bright sunshine and high pressure would put the fish under the docks. Everybody else must have had the same idea, including some local fishermen. Dock after dock was covered up. All the guys were running the same stretches of docks. Consequently, I never had another bite the rest of the day.

I arrived at the weigh-in at 4:37 p.m. I was seven minutes late. They gave me the wrong time. My own fault though. I knew better. I should have believed in myself.

It cost me my one 2-pound fish that I worked all day to catch. You just can't imagine how discouraging it is not only to not catch any fish, but then to have circumstances take the one fish away that you worked so hard to catch. It doesn't mean anything here at this tournament, but 2 pounds could make a lot of difference at the end of the year. I've missed the Classic several times by less than 2 pounds.

I'm very discouraged with myself. Diane and I drove straight home without talking much at all. I didn't even let her drive. I drove all the way in. A lot of times, driving helps me to take out my frustrations and unwind. I just wear myself down.

Winning Ways

David Wharton had never seen Lake Murray before the tournament came to town. But he soon learned that the hottest lure among local anglers was a white floating worm. That weightless worm produced well enough on the final day to secure his second B.A.S.S. win. The bulk of Wharton's 48 pounds, 12 ounces came on a 5 1/2-inch Ditto Gator Tail plastic worm rigged Texas style on 12-pound test line with a 1/4-ounce Gambler Florida Rig self-pegging bullet weight. His primary pattern revolved around fishing two large patches of elodea (a milfoil-like vegetation) at a mid-depth range. He concentrated on a 200-yard stretch of shoreline vegetation that gradually dropped from 5 to 12 feet and a long tapered point where the elodea stopped growing at the 12-foot mark.

We ended up finally getting home about 3:30 a.m. I had been up almost 24 hours. I'm exhausted mentally and physically. I guess all I can do is just once again re-group and try to be better prepared for the next tournament. And concentrate on executing and making no mental mistakes. That's my goal for the next one.

I have to get back into the swing of things. Inside it's killing me. I have to make things turn around.

Chapter 5

The Coldest Place
On Earth

Oklahoma Bassmaster Invitational
November 6-8, 1992
Grand Lake

OCTOBER 31st

We spent all day driving to Tulsa on our way to a meeting at the offices of Lowrance Electronics. I stopped at Zebco and dropped my boat off at about 4 p.m. I met with Rick Scott for about an hour and discussed a lot of sponsor-type matters and visited a little bit. It's rare that we get to visit the plant. It was kind of nice to just sit and talk to him without it being over the telephone.

We checked into our hotel in Tulsa where we'll be staying for two days. The first day we will be meeting with Lowrance and the second day will be meetings with Zebco. There are award banquets each night. Then it's off to Grand Lake for the Bassmaster Oklahoma Invitational.

NOVEMBER 1st

I spent all day doing a factory tour of Lowrance Electronics in Tulsa. Meetings all day, even with Darrell Lowrance in the afternoon. We discussed new products, advertising possibilities, the direction the company is heading, and basically how utilization of the pro team is going to be done.

I feel good about the Lowrance pro team and the longevity of it. I think that the company is behind it and it's going to stay around for a while.

I went back to the hotel at 6 p.m. and had to be at the Country Club in Tulsa for the Zebco awards dinner at 7. I was surprised to get an award from Zebco for winning the 1990 Red Man All American. It's been a while since I won that. They awarded a plaque to several anglers who had won major tournaments. It's a beautiful plaque with an etched portrait in it. I also received a gold diamond ring, which denotes my affiliation with Zebco and the tournament that I won. They'll add a diamond each time I win a tournament.

It was kind of neat. I really feel like I'm a part of the Zebco program now.

In bed at 10:00 p.m.

NOVEMBER 2nd

The day began with breakfast at Zebco at 7:30 a.m. All day meetings followed to go over new products and advertising campaigns and how they will utilize the pro team.

Diane met me there at Zebco at 3 p.m. We hooked up the van to the boat and headed for Grand Lake. We stopped in Tulsa at the Okie Bug tackle store. Bought a license and watched the 10-pound-plus bass living in their big 10,000-gallon aquarium. That was really something to see.

The temperature has become very drastic. The snow is falling right now. The wind chill is well below zero. I think the actual temperature is about 18 degrees outside.

Tomorrow is the first day of practice on Grand Lake. I'm really apprehensive about it. Everything I have is frozen. Diane and I spent about 30 minutes at a gas station spraying de-icer into our locks and trying to get every thing broken loose so I can just get in to my rod locker for my tackle.

At the hotel, we realized that there was really no place to charge your batteries unless you pay them $25 to park in a parking lot where they've got electricity or rent a boat slip. The weather being the way it is, I'm afraid we might not be able to get our boats in and out of the water, with the ice freezing on the ramp. So I elected to get a boat slip. An uncovered slip for $45 for the week seemed like a bargain. In the snow and freezing ice, we put the boat in the water and brought all of the gear to the room. It was just a real hassle. A beautiful place, though. But it's a real hassle having to take your gear up four flights.

According to the forecast tonight, it's supposed to go down to 10 degrees tomorrow. I'm really worried about practice tomorrow.

Zebco president Jim Dawson presented me with a special team member plaque.

I'm going to go out there and do it.

NOVEMBER 3rd

First practice day. Because of the freezing temperature, I didn't even go out until 8 a.m. I still think I was one of the few guys that even went out at all.

The temperature when I woke up this morning was 12 degrees with a minus-10 degree wind chill. Even with gloves and the snowmobile suit and the long underwear and everything, it was still very hard to function. Just moving around the boat was very difficult.

I fished right around Shangri La Resort most of the day, which is where I'm staying at the tournament headquarters. It was just too bitterly cold to run.

I fished Honey Creek and several pockets nearby. Fishing was surprisingly good though. Water temperature is 52 degrees. We have bright, clear, sunny skies — I don't know what we would have done if it would have been cloudy. I don't think we could have stood it. The high temperature of the day was 28 degrees.

The ice kept freezing on my rod guides all day. One of the most difficult things was keeping the ice off of the level-wind of my reel.

Basically, this is an old, old lake. The only cover in the water, really, is man-made cover. Brushpiles and docks. Most of the points, banks and channels are all gradually sloping. The backs of the creeks are silted in. Because of the severe weather we've had, the back ends of the creeks are especially cold. The most stable water, temperature-wise, is near the main lake where I found the water temperature to be around 52. The backs of the creeks are somewhere around 47 to 48 degrees.

Mostly today, I fished boat docks and nearby brushpiles, trying to keep my boat in about 10 feet of water. The bass seem to be pretty shallow. I caught a 4-pounder and one other keeper on a crawfish-colored Bass Magnet, casting it around the edges of docks. I shook off several other fish that hit a 1/2-ounce pumpkinseed jig with a pumpkin crawfish trailer (on 14-pound line). Just pitching it and skipping it up under docks and right in to the middle of the brushpiles. The fish are definitely holding tight to the cover.

The bass haven't made their deep water movement yet. The fish that have been up shallow are still shallow, just tight to the cover. I also noticed that the 45-degree sloping banks seemed to be the best. I didn't get very many bites on bluffs and I didn't get very many bites on flat banks.

I persevered until about 4:30 p.m. Diane fixed dinner in our kitchenette. Richard Everett, my practice partner and friend from Odessa, Texas, joined us for dinner. Then it was time to go to registration.

The cold really plays havoc on you. It makes you very tired. I'm going to turn in as early as I can.

NOVEMBER 4th

Second day of practice. I got out an hour earlier today. The temperature wasn't quite as severe as yesterday. It was 17 degrees instead of 12 like yesterday. The wind had subsided a little bit.

I decided to fish about 10 miles up the lake today — in the area of Wolf Creek, Elk River and Hickory Hollow. Once again, I caught most of my fish early in the morning. Again, cranking a deep-running crankbait. I caught two fish in the 3-pound category by skipping and pitching a jig around the boat docks. I later caught another one about 3 pounds and another one about 2 pounds and then shook off several fish.

I finished the day out with six or seven bites. But most of them came in the morning. I didn't get very many bites in the afternoon.

I just can't really pinpoint what these fish are doing. I know there are a lot of fish around the brush and the docks, but just about every cove has a similar-minded tournament angler fishing it. They are all fishing the same stuff. I don't think the fish can handle that kind of pressure.

De-icing the compartment latches on my boat.

I've tried some other things, attempting to establish any other type of pattern. I've cranked points and fished channel banks in the back of pockets. I cranked flat points. I can't get a strike anywhere but around the docks. That makes sense, though, this time of year. They are going to be in shallow shoreline cover like docks and brush. Hopefully, I'll be able to find enough good dock areas to run during the tournament.

I fished until 5 p.m. Diane had some hot soup ready and we ate dinner.

I went to the Lowrance get-together at the Shangri La Lodge. A lot of the fishermen were there. We just kind of socialized with everybody.

It's 9 p.m. now, bed time.

NOVEMBER 5th

Third day of practice. Today was a little bit different than the other two days of practice. That's because the weather was different. It was overcast and windy. The temperature was not as severe today as it was the previous two days of practice. The low this morning was in the mid-30s. The high today was somewhere around 50. The wind blew throughout the day. It was pretty severe at times.

With the overcast, instead of fishing docks and brushpiles with a jig and crankbait, I opted for a more shallow, faster approach. I fished a lot of water today using a 1/2-ounce Stanley Vibra-Shaft spinnerbait. I figured if there was ever a day that they were going to come up and bite a spinnerbait, it was today with the heavy overcast.

They did. I caught one of the biggest stringers I've caught in practice in a long time. My first fish was a 3-pounder, which came at 7:30 this morning on a brushpile near a dock. I began running a lot of wind-blown, shallow pockets. Fishing the spinnerbait about a foot under the surface, several times I saw the fish come up and nail it.

My next bass was about 4 pounds, followed by a 5-pounder. I managed to catch several large fish in the afternoon off of shallow brush. One was about 6 1/2 pounds and another one was about 5.

I ended up my day by doing something a little unique. I fished main river bluffs. I knew I had to get away from the crowd. Every pocket or cove that you pull in to has got a boat in it. Everybody is fishing the docks. Relentlessly beating the docks. I tried to find something that wasn't getting pounded quite as hard, so I fished the main river channel bluff walls, which is a good fall pattern. I was keeping my boat very close to the wall, making long casts and just slow-rolling the spinnerbait down. I caught a couple fish in the 4- to 5 -pound range doing that in short order.

Of all the things that I've seen this week that is the pattern that excites me the most. It's something I don't think very many people are doing. It's a kind of pattern — if it holds up — that could very easily be a winner.

So I feel pretty comfortable with what I've found. At the partner pairings meeting, though, I was either fortunate or unfortunate enough to draw Denny Brauer. Denny's catching quite a few fish also. Lately it seems that anytime I'm catching fish, I draw somebody who is also catching fish.

Denny really wanted to use his boat and I guess I'm going to ride with him basically out of respect. Denny's done a lot in the business. He's a very good fisherman. I just kind of felt obliged to ride with him. This may not be a good decision. We'll see tomorrow. He's catching all his fish on a 3/8-ounce black-and-blue jig in 8 to 12 feet of water around docks.

We came back from the meeting at 7:30 p.m. After changing line, sharpening hooks and tying on lures for tomorrow, I'm ready for bed at 9 p.m.

NOVEMBER 6th

First day of competition. And another disappointing day. How many more am I going to have? I fished with Denny Brauer; he is a great fisherman, no doubt. We fished out of his boat. The little problem we had was his fishing technique and mine were totally different for this tournament. He had been catching his fish by slowly working a jig under boat docks and I have been catching all mine

The coldest bass I've ever caught.

moving quite fast along the short pockets against the bluff walls with spinnerbaits, as I described before.

We went to his area and fished a jig for about four and a half hours. Denny managed to catch two small keepers and I caught several undersized fish. But the weather was pleasant and the sky was overcast — making it more conducive to my way of fishing. When his area didn't quite pan out, we moved and began throwing a spinnerbait on the bluff walls. Denny caught a bass weighing about 5 1/2 pounds off the bluff and then a smaller one.

His four fish end up weighing 9 pounds. I did not have a keeper bite all day, but I don't know why. I was doing the same thing right beside him. That just happens sometimes.

I drew Mickey Trousdale from New Mexico for tomorrow. His area isn't producing. So he's willing to ride with me and use my boat for tomorrow. I'm hoping it will be cloudy in the morning and I'll get a chance to do what I feel comfortable doing.

The weather is rapidly getting colder, deteriorating every hour and I wonder if the dropping water temperature is going to turn the fish off that spinnerbait. I'll just have to hope it won't. They're predicting some of the worst weather of the year tomorrow.

I just have to be ready for it to try and catch up. There were some big stringers of fish caught today. A zero on the first day was not good. I've got to snap out of it sooner or later. Maybe tomorrow is the day.

We're staying with a couple of other fishermen and splitting the cost of a big condo. Diane is cooking for everybody. So she cooked dinner, I did my tackle and we went to the Fellowship of Christian Anglers meeting. I got in bed about 9:30 p.m.

NOVEMBER 7th

Second day of competition and probably the coldest day I ever spent in a bass boat. The temperature never got above 28 degrees all day long. It spit snow and sleet all day. Cloudy, overcast, miserable, just as cold as you can imagine and about a 25-m.p.h. northeast wind. A lot of the anglers called it quits and came in early during the day. Mickey was very upbeat, though. And he hung in there even though his hands got pretty cold a couple of times during the day. I'm fishing all day with wool gloves on, a hood over my head, a face mask and a Yamaha snowsuit just to stay warm.

I had some snowmobile boots sent by Federal Express to me by Diane's father, so I've been pretty warm considering the arctic-like conditions. The main problem we had today was the water freezing in the slot where the trolling motor drops in and locks into place. I had some de-icer with me, thank goodness, and was able to free my trolling motor bracket and keep the ice off for at least half of the day. It was very difficult. Rod guides and our reels were frozen constantly.

The temperatures never got any higher. I threw a spinnerbait in the shallow pockets and every place that I had caught fish before. By noon I had not had a bite. Then my trolling motor cable broke. I started to install my hand-oper-

ated trolling motor and attempt to continue fishing, but my front deck was completely coated with ice that I was afraid to be standing up on top of that trolling motor with one foot. It would not have been a very safe situation. I came in and we located the MotorGuide repairman and he put a new trolling motor on. The whole ordeal cost me about an hour and a half of fishing time.

I ran across the lake with about an hour to fish and managed to catch a bass weighing about 2 1/2 pounds and a pair of short fish by paralleling a bluff with docks and brush. This was typical of what I had done all day without success. I guess the area is everything. I just had to be in the right place at the right time.

One fish after two days is not too inspiring. I've been trying to analyze what's going wrong. It's really hard to do that when the weather keeps deteriorating as rapidly as it is.

My partner for tomorrow is Lendell Martin, who fished today with Denny Brauer, my first-round partner. Today, Denny went to the same boat docks he and I fished the day before and caught one of the biggest stringers of the tournament — about 22 pounds. It kind of adds insult to injury. Some of Brauer's biggest fish came off of Lendell's spots, which is where we will spend some time tomorrow.

It's going to be bright, sunny and very cold. I'm going to ride with Lendell.

Right now, I'm very cold, very tired and miserable. I'm going to get something to eat and hit the hay early.

NOVEMBER 8th

Third day of competition. Lendell and I fished the lower end of the lake nearly all day in the midst of a lot of boat traffic. A lot of guys were down there fishing around those boat docks.

Winning Ways

Despite the severe conditions, Ron Shuffield managed to catch 49 pounds, 1 ounce, by pitching a 1/2-ounce black-and-blue Stanley jig with a similar No. 11 Uncle Josh pork frog trailer around docks. These docks are located on a bluff or other steep bank. "The cold made it more of an endurance test than a tournament," he says. "I had to overcome the cold mentally and physically. I've never fished under these conditions in a tournament before."

Using a jig, we both managed to catch two keepers each that totalled about 4 pounds. We committed ourselves to that way of fishing and stayed with it. Lendell was good to fish with. We worked real hard together, but we could only come up with a couple of fish apiece.

The catches were down — except for Ron Shuffield, who won the tournament with a stringer of 49 pounds. It took 13 pounds to make the money in the tournament; I had 6 pounds, 5 ounces.

Diane pulled my boat out during the day. The boat ramp has been icing up so she pulled it out early. Then we headed for Tulsa and another meeting with Zebco.

It will be 13 days and stops at Sam Rayburn Reservoir in Texas and Lake Lanier in Georgia — along with meetings with various sponsors along the way — before I will be home in Ohio. Then I'll have 10 days or so to get things in order and a little time to celebrate Thanksgiving before the tournament trail resumes at Lanier.

Mentally it's really hard to stay psyched when you're performing as poorly as I am and still having to do all these sponsor functions and travel all over the country. About 4,500 miles of driving on my vehicle and my body coupled with poor fishing conditions doesn't help my outlook. I'm hoping that this Thanksgiving period and a little deer hunting with friends will recharge my batteries.

Chapter 6

Minute-By-Minute View Of Big-League Bass

Georgia Bassmaster Top 100
December 4-7, 1991
Lake Sidney Lanier

Editor's Note: The format of this chapter was designed to give the reader a minute-by-minute look at a major-league bass tournament. Instead of dictating a daily report into a tape recorder, Joe Thomas maintained a log of the various activities of the day — on and off of the water. The result is an insider's view of the tournament day, ranging from the most important strategic moves to the most mundane aspects of tournament fishing.

On another note, just before making the drive to Lake Lanier near Atlanta, Joe learned that wife Diane was pregnant with their first child. It was news that would impact his emotions throughout the rest of the season.

NOVEMBER 29th
7:30 a.m. — Wake up.
8 a.m. — Pack van and hook up boat.
11 a.m. — Fill van with gas, check tires and oil.

11:15 a.m. — Drive to Canton, Ga.

3:45 p.m. — Blew trailer tire in downtown Knoxville at 75 m.p.h.. Stopped and changed tire.

7:30 p.m. — Arrive at Claude (Fish) Fishburne's house. Talk briefly about Lake Lanier.

8 p.m. — Fishburne and I have dinner at Fridays in Roswell.

10 p.m. — Watch TV and talk more about Lanier.

11 p.m. — Bed time.

NOVEMBER 30th

8 a.m. —Wake up.

8:30 a.m. — Clean inside of van from blown tire. Tools everywhere.

9 a.m. — Go over finesse tackle and split some with Fishburne.

9:45 a.m. — Drive to Roswell to get new tire for trailer. Lucky, I got the last one the guy had.

11 a.m. — Drive to Suwannee. Check into Days Inn, my home for the week.

11:15 a.m. — Unpack gear into room. Randy Moseley, my roommate, arrives.

1 p.m. — Begin to prepare tackle. Spool new line, sharpen hooks, tie on lures.

3:35 p.m. — Wipe down boat, top off oil, put charger on, re-tighten new wheel.

5:30 p.m. — Take a shower.

6:15 p.m. — Eat at Denny's beside hotel — my usual grilled chicken breast and veggies.

7 p.m. — Go over map and decide practice strategy according to weather forecast.

8:15 p.m. — Rick Van Tiem calls. He's an amateur from Michigan. He will practice with me tomorrow. I met him at a sport show in Detroit.

9 p.m. — Call home. Give Diane the number where I'm staying.

9:30 p.m. — Bedtime. I'm wasted.

DECEMBER 1st

5:30 a.m. — Wake up call. Sky overcast, 40-percent chance rain, 62-degree temperature.

6 a.m. — Rick arrives, unhook charger, grab some ice and head for Gainesville.

6:45 a.m. — Arrive at launch ramp just before light at the mouth of the Chestatee River. Plan to fish for largemouths since it's overcast. They should bite today.

7 a.m. — Launch the boat.

7:15 a.m. — Begin fishing shallow clay points with spinnerbait and Rat-L-Trap.

9 a.m. — No bites yet. Run several miles up Chestatee to headwaters.

9:40 a.m. — First bite of day 14-inch largemouth on a willowleaf spinnerbait from a shallow brush pile next to a dock.

10 a.m. — Fish No. 2 is a 13-inch spotted bass, same spinnerbait, chartreuse and white 1/2-ounce, again from shallow brush.

11:30 a.m. — No more bites on spinnerbait. Can't make pattern work. 61-degree water.

Noon — Begin fishing brown jig- and-pig and pitching it to laydowns and docks.

12:20 a.m. — Catch 5-pound largemouth on laydown tree in 3-foot of water. Nice one.

1:30 p.m. — No more bites on jig so far.

2:30 p.m. — Catch two small non-keepers on crawfish-colored Bass Magnet crankbait.

3:15 p.m. — Catch 2 1/2-pounder on jig beside dock. No pattern to this.

4 p.m. — Run back down towards the main lake to doodle docks with a 4-inch worm.

4:20 p.m. — Catch a 12-inch spot under dock on bottom in 20-feet of water — typical Lanier pattern.

5:51 p.m. — Dark. Load boat on trailer.

6:10 p.m. — Drive back to Suwannee.

7 p.m. — Hook up charger and stow gear.

7:15 p.m. — Shower and change.

7:40 p.m. — Dinner at Denny's again. It's close and it's reasonable.

8:30 p.m. — Call home. Go over some sponsor business with Diane.

9 p.m. — Go over map, talk with Randy. His day was not good either. Bedtime.

DECEMBER 2nd

6 a.m. — Get up. Dress.

6:15 a.m. — Unhook charger, load tackle. Pat Van Tiem, my practice partner (Rick's brother), arrives.

6:25 a.m. — Fill boat with gas.

6:35 a.m. — Drive to Big Creek launch ramp on lower end of lake where tournament will be held.

6:55 a.m. — Launch. Temperature 61 (air), cloudy and calm. Great fishing day.

Strategy: Since the river seemed unpredictable I have decided to spend the second practice day fishing for spotted bass with 6-pound line and a 4-inch worm, 3/16-ounce brass sinker and a glass bead doodling near and under boat docks. This is a very consistent pattern on Lake Lanier.

7:05 a.m. — Begin fishing docks in the Shoal Creek area.

8:10 a.m. — First bite, a 14-inch spotted bass.

8:30 a.m. — Bite No. 2 shakes off in about 18 feet of water near main lake.

9:05 a.m. — Shook off bite No. 3. Almost same depth as No. 2.

10 a.m. — Bite No. 4 same depth and same type. Location near creek mouth. We have a pattern, it appears.

11:30 a.m. — Had nearly 15 bites following the same pattern throughout the day. I feel very confident this is a good way to catch 10 pounds a day.

5:45 p.m. — Pull boat out.

6:30 p.m. — Hook up charger and stow gear.

6:50 p.m. — Shower and change.

7:30 p.m. — Eat at Wendy's.

8 p.m. — Go to Holiday Inn to register for Tournament with B.A.S.S. staff. Crowded.

8:30 p.m. — Go back to room and watch Lethal Weapon II on TV.

9:10 p.m. — Call Diane. She gives me the number of a sport show promoter I must call.

9:30 p.m. — Call show promoter.

9:45 p.m. — Go to sleep.

DECEMBER 3rd

6 a.m. — Wake up call.

6:10 a.m. — Dress and go to boat. I'm practicing by myself today. It's pouring rain and the temperatures are forecasted to fall into the 30s by night. Lovely!

6:25 a.m. — Gas boat.

6:30 a.m. — Drive to Big Creek launch.

6:55 a.m. — Drop boat in.

7 a.m. — The wind is so strong. 10-20 northeast.

7:05 a.m. — Put on a Polar fleece coat under my rainsuit. It's already chilly.

7:15 a.m. — Throw a spinnerbait for two hours on shallow clear water points. The conditions are perfect, but no bites. I don't understand it.

9:20 a.m. — Begin doodling a worm like yesterday in Lan Mar Marina. Got five bites in 18 to 25 feet of water in one hour, using a

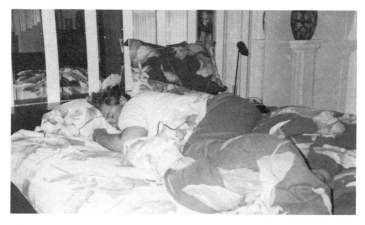

The wake-up call comes early on the tournament trail. Sleep is a precious commodity.

watermelon worm with black flake. They like dark colors when it's cloudy.

11 a.m. — Set the hook on first fish. It's a 2-pounder. This dock thing really works.

2 p.m. — Have gotten nine bites in past four hours. I'm soaked and shivering.

2:15 p.m. — Head for the dock. Haven't come in this early from practice in years. I notice so is everyone else. It's really cold.

2:20 p.m. — Pull boat out.

2:40 p.m. — Gas boat.

2:55 p.m. — Hook up charger. Take clothes and tackle into room to dry. Crank up heat.

3:15 p.m. — Shower forever trying to warm up.

4 p.m. — Work on tackle and watch the weather and news on TV. They are predicting record cold, sun and high winds. My dock pattern should be the hot set-up. Because I'm out of the wind, deep fish are usually stable, and the sun should put them under the docks, not around them. IT'S MY TURN!

6 p.m. — Eat at Denny's.

6:30 p.m. — Go to partner draw at the Holiday Inn.

7:15 p.m. — Get partner. I am boat number 8.

8 p.m. — Final check on tackle.

8:30 p.m. — Call Diane. She wishes me luck.

8:45 p.m. — Sleep.

DECEMBER 4th

4:45 a.m. — Wake up and dress.

6:15 a.m. — Unhook charger. Meet partner and load his gear. It's 26 degrees with 30 m.p.h. northeast winds. Everything is frozen. Have to use hot water to thaw locks on rod lockers. It reminds me of Oklahoma.

6:25 a.m. — Drive to launch ramp at Big Creek.

6:40 a.m. — Break out the snow mobile suit.

6:45 a.m. — Launch boat.

6:50 a.m. — Run to Holiday Marina for blast-off.

6:55 a.m. — Tripp Weldon, the assistant tournament director lines us up in starting order.

7:15 a.m. — Kill switches checked and we get our numbered flag and blast off.

7:20 a.m. — I head north across the lake to what I feel is my best protected area: Lan Mar Marina. Waves are 2 to 4 feet and erratic.

7:35 a.m. — Begin fishing on my best row of marina slips.

7:50 a.m. — First bite. Nice 2-pounder, but he is across a steel bar and breaks off when the line touches it. Tough break.

8:10 a.m. — Move to another line of slips.

8:20 a.m. — Hook another bass. Get about three cranks on him and he pulls off. I had not counted on this.

8:50 a.m. — Move to another marina about a mile away heading towards the dam.

9:05 a.m. — Hook No. 3. It pulls off after several turns of the reel. What's going on?

9:20 a.m. — No. 4 gets almost to the boat before making a short run and pulling off. I've lost 6 pounds or so and have not landed a bass.

9:45 a.m. — Partner hooks and lands a spot from the back of the boat about one and a half pounds.

10 a.m. — Proceed down the lake to some isolated docks and begin systematically running them with my doodling technique.

10:35 a.m. — Change to a silver worm with flake because the sun is now very bright and it is usually most effective in bright conditions.

12:10 p.m. — Hook a nice fish only to have him break off on the ladder of a dock. Obviously I need to be using heavier line.

1:05 p.m. — Hook No. 6. He is off in five seconds.

2:10 p.m. Hook No. 7, about one and a half pounds. Get him to the surface only to have him come off as I am swinging him in. Get the gun.

2:35 p.m. — I boat my first fish from a shallow dock. A large-mouth, if you can believe that, about one and a half pounds.

2:45 p.m. — Hook a real nice one under a deep dock in 10-feet of water. Fight him all over only to have him come off at the surface!

2:57 p.m. — Sprint to weigh in. So disappointed!

3:02 p.m. — Bag and weigh fish.

3:10 p.m. — Meet next day's partner.

3:25 p.m. — Load boat and head for the hotel.

3:50 p.m. — Gas boat. Partner gives me $10 for gas.

4 p.m. — Hook up charger and stow gear. Put on running lights for morning.

4:20 p.m. — Shower and change.

5 p.m. — Call Diane and tell her of my miserable performance.

5:10 p.m. — Work on tackle for next day. Change from 6- to 8-pound line and go to a slightly larger hook. I've got to do something to put these fish in the boat. I'm getting plenty of bites, but I have given away an easy 10-pound catch.

5:50 p.m. — Randy Moseley and I drove to Rich Tauber and Bernie Schultz' room to eat a pizza and watch Point Break on Pay Per View TV. Just trying to break the monotony. We all did lousy.

8:30 p.m. — Back to the room and bed.

DECEMBER 5th

5:45 a.m. — Wake up and dress.

6 a.m. — Meet partner and load his gear. Unhook charger.

6:15 a.m. — Drive to ramp. It's sunny and cold. About 29 degrees, but not as windy.

6:25 a.m. — Launch.

6:30 a.m. — Run to Holiday and stage for takeoff.

6:40 a.m. — Fine-tune tackle and check everything.

6:50 a.m. — Relax until take off.

7:25 a.m. — Get flag and take off.

7:35 a.m. — Run to back of Big Creek and begin fishing docks in 15-25 feet of water.

8:15 a.m. — First strike. About 10 inches long. Throw back.

8:40 a.m. — Strike No. 2 is just under 12 inches. Throw him back. At least I'm hooking them. Maybe the new hook is working.

9:50 a.m. — Boat a keeper, barely, off shallow dock.

10:15 a.m. — Run to Aqualand Marina. Had shaken off several there in practice.

10:40 a.m. — Miss bite in 18 feet of water. Get back half a worm.

11:15 a.m. — Hook a nice bass in 20 feet. He shakes free near the surface.

11:25 a.m. — Hook and land 1 1/2-pound spot under a sailboat in 22 feet of water.1

12:20 p.m. — Pull up trolling motor and run to Lan Mar Marina.

12:55 p.m. — Lose two bass over 2 pounds on back-to-back casts in the same boat stall after fighting them halfway back to the boat. I lose my cool momentarily.

1:30 p.m. — Catch a 1 1/2-pounder between a houseboat and a dock.

1:55 p.m. — Boat a 1-pound keeper on the other side of the cove.

2:35 p.m. — Hook and lose a keeper across a rope tied to a cruiser.

2:50 p.m. — Boat my last keeper and head for weigh in.

3:20 p.m. — Weigh in 5 pounds, 6 ounces. Miserable. Two- day total of about 7 pounds.

3:30 p.m. — Meet partner and discuss next day.

3:40 p.m. — Load boat.

4:05 p.m. — Gas boat and drop off partner.

4:15 p.m. — Hook up charger and stow gear.

4:30 p.m. — Shower, shave and change.

5:05 p.m. — Work on tackle. Switch to a longer rod, 6 1/2 feet and from a 1/0 to a 2/0 hook. This has to work.

5:50 p.m. — Call Diane and my father to let them know how things are going.

6 p.m. — Dinner at Denny's. Again!

6:30 p.m. — Attend the Fellowship of Christian Anglers meeting at Holiday Inn. I ride with David Gregg of Texas.

7:30 p.m. — Back to hotel.

7:40 p.m. — Watch TV for a while to unwind.

9 p.m. — Bedtime.

DECEMBER 6th

4:45 a.m. — Wake and dress. Temperature still below freezing and clear skies. No wind.

6:15 a.m. — Meet partner. Load gear. He is an observer (a volunteer to make the tournament field even). Unhook charger and head to ramp.

6:40 a.m. — Launch boat.

6:45 a.m. — Proceed to take off at Holiday.

7:00 a.m. — Check tackle one last time.

7:10 a.m. — Relax.

7:28 a.m. — Check out and run to Lan Mar Marina, where most of my fish have come from.

Bass and bitter cold — shades of Oklahoma.

7:40 a.m. — Decide to stop short of Lan Mar and fish a spinnerbait on some main lake points until the sun gets up. Rich Tauber had caught two large spots the day before on a blade in the morning light.

9:10 a.m. — No bites on spinnerbait. Proceed to Lan Mar Marina to doodle worm.

9:20 a.m. — Catch first fish of day, 1 1/2- pound spot in 18 feet of water in open stall.

9:28 a.m. — Land No. 2, just a keeper, two slips farther.

9:50 a.m. — Move to new section of marina where I had lost two bass the day before.

10:05 a.m. — Boat a 2-pound spot from beneath a cruiser in 22 feet.

10:10 a.m. — Land another 2-pounder in the very next slip. I'm finally getting them. The larger hook and rod are doing the trick.

1:45 p.m. — Lose a nice fish deep under a dock.

1:55 p.m. — Catch a 1 1/2-pounder from a slip over a rope. Took a lot of work, but I got this one.

2:15 p.m. — Land another small spotted bass between a houseboat and the dock. Just enough room to get the fish out. I'm finally getting some breaks.

3:05 p.m. — No more bites in marina, so I run to some isolated docks.

3:10 p.m. — Catch the biggest fish of the day and immediately head for weigh in with a seven-bass limit.

3:30 p.m. — Check in.

3:40 p.m. — Weigh fish in at 11 pounds, 6 ounces. Pretty fair catch.

3:55 p.m. — Meet tomorrow's partner.

4:15 p.m. — Load boat.

4:55 p.m. — Gas boat.

5:05 p.m. — Hook up charger and stow gear.

5:30 p.m. — Shower and change into sweats.

5:40 p.m. — Prepare tackle for tomorrow. New line and hooks. Restock my tackle box with silver worms.

6:30 p.m. — Begin to pack van for check out in the morning.

7:00 p.m. — Pick up chicken sandwich at Wendy's and went to Holiday Inn to visit Rich Tauber for a while to discuss our day.

8:45 p.m. — Back to my room.

9 p.m. — Call Diane. Go to bed. I'll be glad to get this one over.

DECEMBER 7th

5:45 a.m. — Wake up and dress.

6:15 a.m. — Finish packing van so that I can take off immediately after the weigh-in today and check out.

6:30 a.m. — Drive to lake.

7 a.m. — Launch boat. Cool, temperature 40 degrees and very foggy.

7:15 a.m. — Meet my partner at gas dock. Can't see anything for the fog.

7:20 a.m. — Fog delay.

10:05 a.m. — Finally, the fog lifts enough for B.A.S.S. officials to release us.

Tournament Tip

Matching the rod, reel, line and bait combination can be one of the most critical factors in determining your fishing efficiency (or the bite-to-catch ratio). Rod length can, at times, be more critical than its stiffness. When fishing fairly deep or making long casts, the long rod will allow you to take up more slack on the hookset than a shorter rod. Also, the heavier the line you use, the less stretch it will have, which translates into more hooking power. Always use the longest rod and heaviest line that the situation will allow.

10:15 a.m. — Arrive at Lan Mar Marina to try and doodle a quick limit.

10:25 a.m. — Miss a bite in 20 feet under a boat.

10:50 a.m. — Catch a good solid keeper. Bit the worm three times before I hooked him.

11:15 a.m. — Land second fish, 1 1/2-pounder, in about the same depth, 18 feet.

11:20 a.m. — Partner lands good keeper.

11:35 a.m. — Idle across cove to some isolated docks.

11:40 a.m. — Lose one. Had hooked in front of dock.

11:45 a.m. — Land a 2-pounder from next dock front on some brush on the bottom.

11:48 a.m. — Partner catches a 1 1/2-pounder from same dock.

12:05 p.m. — Cross back to marina docks. No bites.

1:30 p.m. — Run up river to isolated docks I had not fished since early November.

1:55 p.m. — Hook and land a small spotted bass from under a pontoon boat.

2:10 p.m. — Land a keeper from a shallow dock, 10 feet or less.

2:30 p.m. — Partner lands third keeper.

2:40 p.m. — I hook and fight a very large spot for almost a minute, only to lose him on a run near the boat.

2:55 p.m. — Catch a 1 1/2-pound spot and break one off on the same dock. Then my

partner lands one from the same dock. It was loaded with brush around it.

3:05 p.m. — Catch another bass and cull from a very deep dock near a bluff wall.

3:20 p.m. — Land my largest bass of the day from a dock by dropping the bait over the ropes and cables. The depth does not seem nearly as important as getting your bait into the shade under the boats or dock.

3:30 p.m. — Partner lands his fifth fish. This will move him way up in the amateur standings.

4 p.m. — Head to weigh-in.

4:10 p.m. — Weight of fish was 9 pounds, 14 ounces. Total for the tournament is 28-6, which wasn't close to the money weights..

Reflection: If I had just gone to a longer rod and bigger hook the first day, my goal of 10 pounds a day would have been no trouble. You can't loose 16 bass and do well!

5:05 p.m. — Load boat.

5:15 p.m. — Get gas, a Mountain Dew and head for home. Lots of time to think and replay the tournament on the eight-hour drive home.

5:20 p.m. — Head for Cincinnati.

1 a.m. — Arrive in Cincinnati exhausted.

Chapter 7

The Art
of
Tournament Fishing

"There's more involved
than just catching fish"

Like any professional sport, tournament bass fishing has evolved into an artform for its most successful performers.

Spend one day in the major leagues of competitive fishing and you will discover that there is more than just catching bass that molds and fashions careers at this level. Much more.

The most successful bass pros have learned to manage all aspects of big-league bass fishing — strategic, political, emotional — so well that they can focus their concentration solely on the actual fishing. Nobody is better at that than Rick Clunn, who could tune out an approaching hurricane.

There are so many considerations, so many decisions involved in the average tournament week. And not all are strategic in nature. Some are more personal like dealing with partners, sponsors, spouses and family. All of it combines to play a part in every tournament.

At times, fooling bass into biting is far easier than controlling the other elements of this occupation.

Here are a few of the aspects of what I like to call The Art of Tournament Fishing.

TO PREFISH OR NOT TO PREFISH

I only prefish the BASS Masters Classic and lakes that I have never been to. Otherwise, I try to stay away from prefishing. I think it can hurt you.

I think if you're familiar enough with a lake, you can find your fish in the three days of official practice before the tournament. Prefishing gives preconceived notions, which can kill you if the bass move during the off-limits period.

BEFORE LEAVING HOME

The first thing is the vehicle. An average tournament is going to be somewhere between 500 and 1,000 miles from your house. So I start out by rotating my tires, checking my oil, servicing my transmission and such.

I then work on my boat — top my oil reservoir off, check the batteries, go through tightening nuts and bolts, all that stuff. Make sure everything is ready to rock and roll. I like to have clean equipment. It presents a good image.

Then I will make sure that I have my maps of the area and the lake. You always have to make sure your motel reservations are made and they are in a comparably convenient place. Not only convenient in terms of location, but financially convenient as well. And I always request a room that is on the first floor. People forget about that. High-rise hotels are not the way to go when you are a bass fisherman. You need a way to get your gear in and out.

I normally will only contact guys that I really trust. If a guy lives on the water and we're friends, I will call and talk to him about what has been going on the last couple of weeks. I want basics and generalities, like water temperature. I don't want detail. Too many guys go to a new lake and they have a friend who has been fishing during off-limits period and will mark a map. Then, in practice, all he does is double-check what his friend has found.

And 90 percent of the time, it will bury him. I want basic, general information.

I usually make sure that I have everything possible as far as clothing is concerned. I prepare for everything from the coldest to hottest weather imaginable. I never take anything for granted. I don't care if it is summertime; I always have cold-weather gear in my boat or vehicle. It stays in my vehicle.

I have a storage system in my vehicle that is designed to be both convenient and ultra-organized. I use large Rubbermaid Action

Packers (the neatest organizing storage boxes ever made) to store my hard lures, soft plastics, line, extra reels, battery chargers and extension cords. The contents of each Action Packer is marked on the outside and lock securely in the boxes. And these storage boxes lay flat, which allows me to put my clothing on top of it. All of that is important.

ARRIVING AT THE TOURNAMENT SITE

I don't like to arrive at a tournament site any later than the day before competition. Most times, that means arriving on Saturday.

I like to roll in there somewhere around noon on Saturday. That way I don't have to pay for an extra night's hotel room. I don't want to sound cheap, but let's face it, if you do it every day, such expenses add up.

A cardinal rule is that I try not to have any commitment (with sponsors or a speaking engagement), if humanly possible, on that Saturday before the first day of practice starts.

I like to spend that time thinking about the tournament, getting my fishing license, spooling line, tying on lures, sharpening hooks and organizing my tackle.

I have different bags of tackle for every area of the country — Ziplock bags with terminal tackle in them that are dedicated specifically to Florida fishing or Georgia fishing. That storage system makes it a lot easier for me once I arrive at the tournament site.

The idea behind this is that you don't have to go and buy six dozen bags of worms just because you're going to Georgia and the tournament is likely to involve finesse fishing. I have the lures I will need still organized in a Ziplock bag from the year before last — or from six years ago.

Let's say we go to Lake Lanier in Georgia. I've got the right color worms. I've got the right sizes. I've got the brass sinkers, the beads, everything that I need for doodling. Everything I need to fish Lake Lanier is in that bag. All I have to do is put it in my boat. It saves time from transferring tackle in and out of tackle boxes.

I spend a lot of time the day before the tournament begins reviewing my lake map, making myself familiar with the launch ramp facilities and basically laying out a game plan for where I will launch every day. I also put together a scheme for each day of practice based on what I want to accomplish.

Re-checking the boat, I fill the gas tank and check everything out just to be sure that it is in good working order. Finally, I charge the batteries.

I also try to unwind a little bit because I have six or seven days of pure heck ahead of me. To me, tournaments are the hardest things I've ever done. Mentally and physically. Finally, I make sure I get a good night's sleep.

A GAME PLAN FOR PRACTICE

In practice, one of the most important aspects is balancing your past experiences on this lake with the current conditions. It's important to use your past experiences to your advantage. But not rely on them so much that it keeps you from opening your eyes to new experiences and opportunities.

Keep your eyes open for new things — what's going on currently. Rarely will one pattern work from one year to the next on a given lake. I do a percentage of reminiscence fishing as a starting point. Seasonal patterns are so important.

One of the things that separates the average guy and a tournament pro is that the average angler usually fishes certain holes, while the pros tend to be pattern fishermen. We don't fish spots, we fish certain patterns. We then attempt to duplicate a pattern in several spots around the lake.

Another major consideration with the practice days is to look at the areas that usually produce the best quality fish. You obviously can't fish all of a massive lake like Rayburn or Okeechobee, but you can often use the lake's history to establish the area where the best bass live.

You can look back on tournament results to get a starting point. Find out what weight won tournaments during that time of year and where the best stringers came from. Don't look for particulars; concentrate on the generalities involved.

I'm told that Rick Clunn has the results of more than 500 tournaments in his computer. He uses this information for gaining a seasonal insight into each body of water.

It's critical to have some place to start. I pick out three general areas that I think I can check out in the three practice days. I usually launch my boat in that area. I try not to run any further than I have to by boat. That allows me to fish later each day.

I try to concentrate solely on one targeted area each day. I try to make the best out of that area or eliminate it completely. That's my goal, anyway.

At the same time, I want to establish a pattern or two in those areas. I try to establish a pattern or two that can be duplicated in other parts of the lake. But while I'm establishing a prevalent pattern for that

Dealing with partners is a crucial aspect of tournament fishing.

day, I remind myself that I need to be open to any changes in the conditions that can signal a switch in strategy.

You have to keep in mind that this is a six-day event — three days of practice and three days of competition. And during that time, you can almost bet that one weather front will pass through. So you have to make considerations in advance of any significant weather change.

If you are catching bass on a buzzbait in the sparse grass, you should have a defined grassline nearby where you can catch them by flipping if the sky gets sunny and bright. If you are cranking a creek channel, you need to have a cover alternative — a place to go flipping if the sun suddenly shines. If there was a sunny sky when you found a group of fish, always look for an area where they are likely to disperse to when an overcast sky appears.

Try to visualize where the bass will go and how you will adjust to that move. Always look for a back-up pattern.

DEALING WITH PARTNERS

So much depends on the partner you draw on each competition day. For each angler to succeed, you have to work together — which isn't always the case. And it goes beyond that. Everybody would want to fish from the comfort of their own boat and have the freedom to go where they want. Nobody likes to share their best spot with another pro of comparable ability who stands beside them on the front deck and gets an equal shot at the best cover or structure.

One bad draw — which could be defined as an uncooperative partner — can cost you an invitation to the big show... the BASS Masters Classic.

That's why I (and most other pros) really enjoy the Bassmaster Top 100 pro-am tournaments. In these events, we have an amateur partner who sits in the back of our boat, has no decision-making power and competes against other amateurs. It doesn't sound nice, but they are at our mercy.

Under this format, the pro is out there on his own. He controls his own destiny. And that's just the way we like it.

In the invitational tournaments, the partner drawing is critical. The more recognized and the better known the angler, the better chance he has of convincing his partner to ride with him in his boat and follow his lead. That's why you rarely see Larry Nixon or Tommy Martin and those guys fishing out of their partner's boat.

In tournaments, boat control and area selection are very critical. Your boat is an extension of you. The way you approach a piece of cover or structure and where you cast is dictated by boat handling. If you are running the trolling motor, you are subconsciously putting yourself in the best position to work that cover. You're not trying to axe out the other guy, but his positioning just isn't quite as important — regardless of what anybody tells you.

If you are in your partner's boat, the tournament rules allow you to run the trolling motor for half of the fishing day. But that only occurs about 2 percent of the time. Nobody ever does it. Both pros fish in front, but the boat owner usually runs his trolling motor.

There's also the convenience and comfort factor. I have everything I need in my boat. If all of a sudden something changes and you need a 1/4-ounce spinnerbait, you are assured of having it. Or if I need a spare prop or spare trolling motor, I've got it in my boat. But a lot of these guys don't have new equipment with a spare for everything. I carry a spare trolling motor, propeller, fuses, bulbs, lights, everything — and tools to change them.

In the invitational tournaments, a lot of times the guys you draw don't have this kind of stuff because they don't fish for a living. Or financially they can't justify having the spare stuff.

Your risk factor goes way up when you are in another person's boat. However, if I draw Rick Clunn, obviously Rick is going to have all the spare gear and know how to change it. I can also trust him in dangerous water situations. Rick has pretty well gone around the block. But that's not true with less experienced fishermen.

A lot of these guys appreciate our experience and many times they will make a concession on the boat, even if they feel that they have the best fishing area. The comment you hear a lot is "I don't mind you using your boat. I just want a fair shot to be able to go to my fish half the day." That's a fair request.

When two partners can't agree on which boat to take or where to fish first, tournament rules call for the flip of a coin. But I am forced to flip for my boat probably 20 percent of the time. But that's because I, like other veteran pros, have learned how to deal with partners.

The first thing you want to do is feel your partner out. You want to see what kind of a person he is and look for little things like eye contact. I can tell when a guy is stroking me from a mile away because I've seen so many partners. Nervous and jumpy partners are usually the worst. That nervousness usually reflects the fact they are unsure and they are afraid of getting screwed over by the pro. Those are the guys that you really have got to watch for.

The other type of partner that makes me nervous is the guy who starts telling me about all of his accomplishments as we are talking in the parking lot. He hasn't said the first thing about how many fish he has caught. Instead, he dwells on what he's done in the past.

The third type that makes me wary is the guy who says "I'm killing them. I'm catching 50 a day and the limits are no problem." Normally what you want to hear is either moderation or quiet confidence. I want to hear: "I think we could work really hard and catch us six or seven a piece. They are likely to weigh 8 to 13 pounds." I want to hear details. I want to hear, "I'm catching them 12 to 14 feet deep on a black-and-blue jig." I don't want to hear generalities about catching 15 fish over here and 22 over there.

I like the guy that can look you in the eye and tell you directly how he feels. Normally, he will be very conservative. I try to treat a partner with dignity and respect. I listen to him, and then I interject my feelings. There is a lot of psychology going on. I try to project confidence without any arrogance. Arrogance is the last thing I want to project. If anything, I want to project humility. You are interested in how he is doing and how he is catching his fish. You think it is great that he is catching them.

But my main concern is to have an opportunity to fish efficiently the areas that I worked three hard days in practice to find. Your partner needs to know that. I'm just going out there to do my job and we'll both catch fish if we remain calm and work together.

83

I know well what a good or bad partner draw can mean to a Classic appearance or a career. One time I made the Classic because of a partner, Jon Hall, who took me to an area where I caught 20 pounds out of the back of his boat. He helped me jump from 6 pounds out to 14 pounds into the 1987 Classic.

Then there was the final tournament of 1988 when I was clinging to a Classic birth by just 2 pounds, 2 ounces. The first day of competition, my partner insisted on using his boat because he had a boat sponsor (like we all do). I was on so many fish that it was painful to lose the coin toss. Boat control and positioning was very critical to the way I was catching those bass. But my partner wouldn't cut me any slack, saying that this was his only B.A.S.S. tournament of the year. It could have been a fantastic day if things had gone right. We both had a mediocre limit early, but he then insisted upon running up the river to his area, where we never caught another bass.

All I had to do was just hang in there and try to cull to improve my limit because the fish were biting. But with him in control of the boat, I was at his mercy.

And I missed the Classic by 9 ounces.

GAMBLING VERSUS CONSERVATIVE

Having the courage to gamble and knowing when to take that chance is a talent reserved for the very best tournament bass pros. Guys like Roland Martin and Denny Brauer are famous for knowing when to abandon one strategy and switch to the tactic that will hit a home run.

I have a tremendous desire to do that, especially when I am behind and wanting to catch up. I find myself trying to hit a grand slam or trying to win it all in one day.

Larry Nixon gave me some good advice when we fished together in a U.S. Open several years ago regarding this subject. He said "If I could only give you one piece of advice, it would be to try to go out and catch a limit every day. Because if you try to go out and catch big fish, they're going to burn you. Big fish just happen. You can't make them happen." Four years later I'm still realizing that.

I've come to believe that he's right, but I still try to make big fish happen. I'll find one little area that has a few big ones in it and I'll think that I can go and make them bite. I'll gamble everything to try and make it happen again, to be a hero. But Larry is right. It's a smarter strategy to catch a limit every day.

When it comes to gambling for a big stringer, the thing that people overlook about guys like Clunn, Brauer and Guido Hibdon is that they have put themselves in the position to win every time before

There is so much involved in tournament fishing before you ever get to make a cast.

they took that gamble. They didn't gamble on the first day. That's very critical. Rick Clunn stresses putting yourself in the position to win first.

Rarely will big fish bite every day. Normally it's a better strategy to try and get yourself into the top 20 and then gamble on catching big bass. That way, if you have a bad day, you are going to fall to 40th place and still take home $1,500. Everything is going to be cool and you're not going to be burned that bad.

The smarter pros limit gambling to the last day of the tournament or to after they've finished off a limit. After you've got a limit, then you can go for the big ones. I know that when I'm flowing the best and things are going well, I don't consciously try to catch a big one. The big bass just happens.

CONCENTRATION: THE OVERLOOKED KEY

The most successful pros have an innate ability to block out all distractions and concentrate fully on the task at hand. When Rick Clunn talks about the mental aspects of fishing, he's referring to the ability to focus on each individual aspect of the cast and retrieve.

This is far easier said than done. Fatigue, harsh weather and frustration all chip away at our ability to concentrate.

During my best years, I have always felt like I am able to focus the best. I block everything else out. My confidence level is so high. Confidence is everything in this game. My confidence level gets so high that I believe everything I do is going to produce a good catch. Conversely, when I start to falter, I start questioning myself and listening to other people (partners in particular).

I start doubting myself. I start changing in mid-stream. That lack of focus and concentration always leads to a lack of success.

Another thing I believe in is physical conditioning. At our level, it is important to be in the kind of physical condition that enables you to concentrate better in a wide variety of weather conditions. Fatigue doesn't set in as much. When you are fatigued, it is hard to concentrate.

I hear guys talk about how tired they are all of the time. And mentally I'm tired at the end of the day. But physically, fishing is not that hard. Climbing a mountain and chasing elk in Wyoming, that's hard. Your lungs feel like they are coming out of your throat.

Rough boat rides will make me a little sore. But I'm in good enough physical shape and I have the proper clothing so that bad weather and rough water rarely gets a second thought. Physical conditioning allows you to ignore fatigue and concentrate. Proper clothing allows you to manage the weather without worrying about it.

Like most pros, I avoid 'dock talk' and exchange information only with a few friends.

TOURNAMENT TALK

Tournament fishermen are among the biggest gossips you'll find anywhere. Rarely does a tournament conclude without most of the field knowing where and how the leaders are fishing.

I try to room as far away from the tournament headquarters as possible, because I am a firm believer that the more input I get — I call it dock talk — the worse I do. We sometimes rent houses or mobile homes away from the lake or stay in different hotels. I try to get to my room without having to converse much with other fishermen.

Dock talk is the worst thing that could happen to you. It usually works against you. But if you are going to listen, it's important to listen for that one little key element that might help you.

I remember overhearing Ken Cook talking to somebody and he mentioned the fact that in his area, the pH didn't get right until afternoon when the sun got on it. It just hit me like a ton of bricks that when I found my fish in this particular canal in that tournament it was afternoon when there was a lot of sunshine. But then I fished it all morning the next day without getting a bite. And I was puzzled. But Ken filled me in on why they didn't bite. The pH was all wrong. So I waited until the afternoon to go in there and I caught them.

Be selective in what you hear and, of course, consider who you are hearing it from. And try to pick out things that will be beneficial to you, that pertain to your pattern — not just general bull that you hear a lot.

Some pros actually work together in practice and share information (and ponder strategy) during the competition days. But many fishermen take the wrong approach in working together.

You wouldn't believe the number of times I have seen two guys bird-dogging each other all day in practice and fishing just 100 yards apart. Working together, in that respect, is not good. But being able to share general information at the end of the day with another good friend is not a bad idea. Rich Tauber and I do that to some extent. I do that with a few select friends.

You need to share information only with those that you trust and know won't be spreading that information around. Trust is everything. I want a person I trust to tell me if I'm missing the boat somewhere. Let's say we are fishing the Harris Chain of Lakes. Lake Griffin may be hot and that's the only lake you haven't been able to check in practice.

You've got to make a decision on where to practice on the last day — Lake Dora or Griffin. That's where Rich might say "Hey, the canals in Griffin are really happening." He doesn't need to say much more than that. I can go find out everything else. He's put me in the right lake, though. That's valuable information.

Chapter 8

A Mid-Season Assessment

Battling a monster called pride

EDITOR'S NOTE: On the eve of the Bassmaster Florida Invitational on the Harris Chain of Lakes in Leesburg, Fla., — the half-way point in the season — Joe Thomas stopped to reflect on the tournaments gone by and those still to come with Tim Tucker. It turned into a conversation that revealed his innermost thoughts on a variety of timely subjects — from his chances of returning to the coveted BASS Masters Classic to the upcoming birth of his first child. In the process, the conversation gives the reader a rare insight into the tournament bass pro, the man and the angler.

Tucker: We come to the half-way point of the season. How would you sum up the first half?

Thomas: It's been a rough time. By my records and my memory, it's far and away the worst start of a season I've ever had. Some of the most discouraging things are that I've had everything from minor equipment failures to changing weather that I didn't adjust well enough to — and even a couple of days where I couldn't keep fish on the hook. So I've had a lot of different things go wrong. I've tried to re-group and figure out what I was doing wrong. There's so many different things going wrong, I don't think it's any one thing that I'm doing. I think I just have to throttle through it.

I took about a month off during the holidays to do a lot of deer hunting and goose hunting. I just didn't think about fishing for a while. And for the first time, I was actually looking forward to going fishing (as the tournament began). It's been a long time since I felt that way. The time off really recharged my batteries. And I'm doing the sport show seminars again and I'll be real honest with you, sometimes you'll get 300 or 400 people show up to see you and that's one thing they can never take away from me. I know how to communicate with people. Whether the fish bite or not, that's one of the abilities that I have.

I keep having to remind myself how lucky I am. And that things *are* good and I have done well over the last two years. I shouldn't let four or five tournaments get me down so much.

Tucker: Some of the things that have happened to you this season are all a part of the sport of fishing.

Thomas: Yeah, they really are. They're all part of the game. I just happened to string eight good tournaments in a row last spring and summer — and now I've strung four or five bad ones in a row.

Tucker: And you've no doubt searched for answers.

Thomas: It's amazing how long I've sat and thought about it. I've kicked myself and I've really gotten down on myself at times. I get a lot of comments while being at the sport shows like "What's your problem, I haven't seen your name" 20 or 30 times a day. I'm human. I just have to tell them that my time will come again. I'm only 30.

People realize that I've been at this nine years. But I've done a lot in nine years. And I have to keep reflecting on that. Nobody is working any harder day after day than I am. I go daylight until dark. I think about things constantly. I'm organized. I'm methodical. It's got to pay off like it has before. It's paid off so many times in the past that I've got to come out on top eventually.

Tucker: Are there any more distractions this year than previous years?

Thomas: No. We've got the baby on the way, but that's not a problem. Actually, the year I got married was the year when all of the good things happened. It really was. Getting married was a good thing. It really settled me down and my fishing improved as a result. The baby was a planned thing. We wanted one and it's coming when we planned. Diane is healthy and everything is fine. I got more support at home than ever before.

I've got the perfect situation. I've got a good income, a good living environment, everything I need and want. I can't say that I have

Diane has been a source of comfort during the tough times so far this season.

lost the killer instinct, though, because it still hurts just as bad when I lose. And I want to win just as bad as I ever did.

Tucker: There's still that monster called pride, too.

Thomas: You better believe it. And that's the hardest thing to swallow. When you get people repeatedly coming up and they beat on you verbally by asking you "what's your problem?" and "what's going on?', the pride monster eats at you a little bit. But I just have to just keep my focus ahead and keep on believing I can catch up. Even though I've had a horrendous start and I'm in 140th place at this time on the Invitational side with a pathetic 15 or 16 pounds, 15th place is just 33 or 34 pounds. So I'm just two good catches out. And I've got to look at it like that. It can still be done. I have to believe that.

Tucker: And we know that you are used to coming from behind and, one way or the other, creating a dramatic finish on the last day every year.

Thomas: Right. We've got some big tournaments coming up. I think this is a critical tournament. I'm not going to fool myself. This is a real critical one because this is the kind of place where there won't be a lot of fish caught — I really believe that. But I believe there will be a few big stringers brought in. There will be some ground made up here. Gosh, if I could just find something a little different...

I ran a pattern today that has paid off when I finished in the top 20 of the last two MegaBucks tournaments here. I went in behind the grassline and used a spinnerbait like Rick Clunn. We fish a lot of the same water here, but Rick has been a little more efficient here and he has finished in the top 10. The water is a lot muddier now and it's 15 degrees colder. I ran that pattern today, a cloudy day when it should have been right. And I got four bites that would have weighed 4 pounds. That was pretty disappointing. I didn't prefish here. I know how to find my way around here. I just have to find out what's going on now. I couldn't see coming down here and prefishing. This is such a changeable time for the bass.

Tucker: Recap for me your last-day heroics in the past and what it was like.

Thomas: Tons of pressure, mainly. Every year but one or two of my nine years on the tournament trail, I was either in the Classic standings or out based on my performance on the last day. There is so much weight on your shoulders going into that final day. It made it pretty awesome when I pulled it off, but it also made it hurt pretty bad when I didn't.

Tucker: What has been the lowest point for you this year?

Thomas: Probably the first day at Oklahoma. On the last day of practice at Grand Lake, I had one of the biggest stringers I've had this year. I had six fish that weighed about 26 pounds. On the first day of competition, I drew Denny Brauer and we had a total conflict in styles. But the weather changed, too. I can't guarantee you that everything would have gone my way had I been on my own. But I still believe I would have done well if I could have dedicated myself to that day and capitalized on what I had found. Denny caught 10 pounds doing basically my thing.

We fished his water early and then my water late. Denny was very, very good about that. There was no conflict at all. But it was a situation where you had to commit to one thing or the other, I think. Denny tried to flex with me and do a little bit of my thing and a little of his thing. He managed to catch 10 pounds, while I blanked right beside him.

That was one of the lowest points. I remember thinking "Here is it. This is where I really need to make my move." I really believed I had a chance to make my move on the invitational side right then. I didn't catch 5 or 6 pounds. I blanked. And that put me even farther behind. That was a low point, but then I went straight to Lake Lanier where on the first competition day I hooked 11 bass and landed *one*. I had almost 30 pounds for the tournament and missed the money by 4 pounds. And I caught 1 pound the first day. That was a pretty low point, too.

And we're doing this book and I try not to think about it, but still I want to do well to make this a good book.

Despite its rewards, tournament fishing can be a lonely profession.

Tucker: You touched on my next question. Do you feel extra pressure because of this book?

Thomas: Truthfully, yes, there is a little bit. Had it started out to be smooth or an average year where I make the money in two out of three events, which is about normal for me, I wouldn't feel any pressure about the book. But you go 0-for-4 or 0-for-5 and things are bad, you're sliding downhill... You could be writing about anybody. I don't want you to be writing about anybody. I want you to be writing about me and a successful year.

But this is the truth. We're just telling the readers the truth. These people want to read the truth about me and the tournament trail. Streaks like these can be a fact of life to almost anybody on the circuit.

At mid-point, things are looking pretty bleak. But maybe we'll have a good ending to this book.

Tucker: What are your feelings about having your first child? That can be pressure of a different kind.

Thomas: The only pressure that I can see probably is more pressure to provide financially. I think a little bit about it — things that I didn't think about before. Adequate life insurance. Savings. I've got a pretty good chunk of change put away. But you're talking about a kid, a wife, a house, college. That's not a lot of money.

I turned 30 and I start thinking about the fact that almost half of my life is gone. A third of my life is spent right here on the tournament circuit. I think back and it has gone so fast. I've got a lot to show for it, but, boy, not nearly as much as I want.

Talking about the baby, I guess I just want to make sure that they have everything that they need and want.

Tucker: It kind of brings things into focus, doesn't it?

Thomas: What it does more than anything is kind of make you realize what's really important and what's really not. If I don't make this Classic and if I don't make the money in a tournament all year, it's not nearly as important as if that baby comes out healthy or not. I think about that.

That's out of my control totally. You think these fish are out of my control — that's *totally* out of my control. So, yeah, it puts things in perspective. And that's good, though.

Chapter 9

The Toughest Event In B.A.S.S. History

Florida Bassmaster Invitational
January 22-24, 1992
Harris Chain of Lakes

JANUARY 18th

Saturday before practice begins. I spent most of that day checking into the room, getting my gear ready, going into town looking for a few baits, buying a fishing license, last-minute tackle preparation and trying to set up a game plan for what I intended to do.

With 325 fishermen in this tournament, fishing the canals would probably be a bad move. There are just so many canals and the boat traffic will be murder. So I plan on fishing out in the main lake, particularly Lake Harris. I hear it's the least affected from all the weed spraying. Supposedly they had a massive fish kill down here and the fishing is brutal. They're not catching very many. And then with this 25-degree cold front on top of things, it's not going to be pleasant.

JANUARY 19th

First day of practice. A friend of mine, Lance Fenlinson from Indianapolis, met me at 5:30 a.m. for the drive into Leesburg and the Venetian Gardens boat ramp. I will fish Lake Harris today. The forecast is for cooling temperatures and clouds. In most of the

MegaBucks tournaments held here, I've done well. I've caught my fish around cypress trees behind the grassline on a spinnerbait. Cloudy conditions are usually most conducive for this kind of fishing.

When we started out this morning it was just overcast and a little breezy. Temperatures were probably in the mid-60s. I caught four fish in the first three hours fishing docks and trees inside the grassline on a 1/2-ounce chartreuse spinnerbait with a No. 5 gold willow-leaf blade. Just dropping it around the cypress trees. I noticed though there's1 not nearly as much water around the cypress trees as there usually is this time of year. I guess they've dropped the water level for some reason. It's definitely very low and it's very stained, nasty looking.

I managed to get four bites the first three hours. And then the rain started coming down and the temperature began to drop rapidly. And it turned into one of the coldest days I've ever spent on the water — and this is Florida. I gave Lance, my partner, every extra set of clothes I had and he was still freezing.

I started to worry about him getting hypothermia because he was shivering so bad that he couldn't fish anymore. I was pretty uncomfortable also, but I stayed out there and fished all day in it without getting another bite. I moved from the cypress trees to the lily pads, which is another good pattern to fish in Lake Harris. I flipped all the lily pads that I could find that were sheltered from the wind.

The water is very cold. It's 58 degrees and falling. I fished until dark and never had another strike. Overall, I had four bass on a spinnerbait and they were all less than 13 inches long. Not a one of them would have weighed a pound. They were very sick, anorexic looking fish.

So I need to try something else. I plan to spend the whole day fishing Lake Griffin tomorrow, especially the mouth of canals and lily pads and the Oklawaha River that feeds it. Maybe that flowing water part of the river has not been poisoned like the lower lake has.

JANUARY 20th

Second day of practice. Fishing is terrible to say the least. Everyone I've talked to had two or less bites the first day of practice. I put in at Lake Griffin and fished with Lance again today. Another cold morning. The skies cleared and the temperature got fairly comfortable in the afternoon.

I've fished every spawning area that I knew on Lake Griffin and three or four good canals. Because it's so sunny I mostly flipped all day long, figuring the fish would be tight to the cover. I flipped reeds and lily pads extensively and got my first bite today at 3:45. It was about a 3-pound fish in a patch of lily pads. I went on to fish every set of lily pads near the mouth of Oklawaha River. Although I didn't get another strike, I'm beginning to believe that these isolated patches of pads in 3 or 4 feet of water could be the hot ticket this week.

But there is a lot of boat traffic up there, so a lot of people must be thinking the same thing.

It's like you're fishing in a lake that's dead. You put your bait in so many good-looking places where you would normally get a bite — and nothing happens. I managed to catch another fish on a black-and-chartreuse plastic crawfish on a 3/8-ounce sinker on 20-pound Stren line.

I flipped for an hour and a half and I had one strike to show for it. It was a 2-pound bass, the last of the day. So I had two bites in two totally unrelated areas and situations. That's not very promising.

I guess I can take comfort in the fact that things are apparently tough for everybody. In a normal B.A.S.S. tournament, the other competitors don't talk much about practice days. But everybody seems dumbfounded. No one I talked with had a strike today. So it's just brutal. I have to wonder if the fish just aren't all dead. Or at least a big percentage of them. The good side of it is that the weather was nicer today. It's supposed to be cold tonight, but a little bit sunnier and nicer tomorrow.

JANUARY 21st

Last practice day. My frustration is at an all-time high.

I put in at Lake Dora at daylight. I went through the Lake Dora canal and began flipping all the best reed patches. I've had some great success in Lake Dora in the past. I know if you slow down and really fish thoroughly you can usually get a couple of bites a day there and they're usually big ones. I spent five hours in Dora with plenty of tournament company. I am really surprised there were that many boats in Dora.

I'm putting my bait in so many good places where the fish ought to be— I can't believe I can't get a bite. I fished most of Lake Dora until about 12:30 p.m. and then finally I moved back through the Dora canal into Lake Eustis. I ran up the east bank, but never had a strike. I moved on around to the mouth of the gator hole in Lake Eustis which is where I caught one of my big stringers a couple of years ago in MegaBucks. I fished basically every lily pad that I could find in 4 or 5 feet of water. Normally that's a good staging or pre-spawning area. I had them to myself for the most part and I couldn't get a bite. How can I formulate a pattern when I can't get a strike?

I got my only strike of the day flipping maidencane in the Haynes Creek canal. So that means I had one bite below the lock in the Haynes Creek canal and now I've had another bite above the lock in the Haynes Creek canal. That's the closest thing to a pattern I've seen. I shook that fish off, but I'm sure it was a bass. I fished until dark.

After changing clothes and working on my tackle, I went to the tournament meeting. When the pairings were announced, I drew a local angler from the Leesburg area who said he had seven bites today. I tried not to be negative, but find that very difficult to believe. Nobody I've talked to has had seven darn bites. How could he have had them? He has been fishing some of the same areas I've worked.

I don't really have anything to go on. I have to give him the benefit of the doubt. I am going to spend a few hours first thing in the morning fishing behind the grass in the trees. He's nice enough to let me use my boat. But he does want to do his thing half of the day.

Fellow Ohio pro Mike Saleeba said he hasn't had a bite in three days of practice either, but got some information from a friend of his. I normally try not to talk to people, but when the situation is this bad, you almost have to take any kind of input you get. Saleeba seems to think a small worm fished slowly in the canals on light line is the best bet. The fish, he feels, in the canals are not very aggressive. Everybody is fishing the cover on the sides of the canals. So slowly fishing the worm away from the cover out in the deep part of the canals might be the hot set-up.

I'm going to keep that in the back of my mind if everything else doesn't seem to pan out right. I've got a couple of canals that are good deep spawning-type canals I could check out and see what happens — maybe in the last couple of hours of the afternoon after the water warms up a little bit. It's supposed to be very cold in the morning and then warm up as the day goes on.

Very apprehensive about tomorrow to say the least. I don't have anything going. I know it's going to be a tough tournament, but I have to try to catch up, so I'll try my best. Maybe I can get a big bite or two out of those lily pads tomorrow.

JANUARY 22nd

First day of competition. My partner is Doug Robinson from nearby Tavares. One of the nicest guys I've drawn for a partner in a long time. But, as I had feared, he wants to fish a lot of the areas that I fished unsuccessfully in practice — and I think we were doing a lot of nostalgic fishing (you know places where he caught them before). They are places where I had caught them before, too, but they just aren't producing now.

The fish were scarce, but there were plenty of fishing fans in Leesburg

We began the day by going in behind the grassline and fishing around the cypress trees with a spinnerbait. We did have a little bit of chop on the water from the wind so it seemed like the thing to do.

After 2 1/2 hours of fishing the trees without a strike, my partner suggested that we try one of the brushpiles that he had planted, as we made our way to Little Lake Harris to fish the lily pads. We pulled up to the first brushpile and I immediately got a bite on a little 4-inch plastic worm with a 3/16-ounce. sinker. When I set the hook there was nothing there — a lot of teeth marks on the worm that looked like a bass had grabbed it. We did not get a strike on his other two brushpiles.

At about 11 p.m., we tried the lily pads in Little Lake Harris and fished them thoroughly for almost three hours without the first hint of action. With a weigh-in time of 4 p.m., I knew we would really have to hustle and do some things differently to pull out this day. So I suggested that we run up to some of the small canals and fish the little worm techniques that I had heard about.

On the way to the Dead River, we stopped to try another one of his brushpiles. Almost immediately, each of us caught a 1 1/4-pound fish off of it — our first two fish of the day — at a little after 1 p.m. Then we headed for a canal off of the Dead River that I knew was a good canal from years past. I went into the open canal and immediately caught an undersized bass which gave us a little bit of inspiration and we fished on through. My partner caught a tiny keeper practically under the boat right out in the middle of the canal which gave us a another lift. The day was running short, though, as we fished through another pair of canals.

With an hour left in the tournament, I suggested we go to the one next to it which was a little deeper. I pulled in to find Mike Folkestad, Homer Humphreys and Larry Williams in there. I picked another canal that didn't have any boats in it and immediately caught a keeper bass about 12 1/2 inches long and an undersized one. I had two fish to my credit with just enough time to run back. I ran a few trees on the way back in the last 15 minutes, but never had another bite.

My two bass for the day weighed 2 pounds, 6 ounces. This was just an ounce out of the top 50 for the first day to give you an idea of how tough the fishing was. Eight pounds is leading after the first day with 315 fishermen. The fishery is just dead, obviously, compared to the weights of the previous years. The weather is not that bad; there should have been a lot of fish caught and there just wasn't.

Like everyone else, I wondered what happened to the bass in the Harris Chain.

For tomorrow, I've drawn a Texas fisherman, who has caught one bass the first day and really doesn't have anywhere to go. So he will follow my advice. I'll head for those few canals that have some fish in them. I'm going to lighten up a little and drop down to 8- or 10-pound test line, a light sinker and run the canals in Dead River. I'm going to stick in the canals all day and see what happens. Obviously it's going to take about 7 or 8 pounds to make the money in this tournament so if I can get 2 or 3 pounds each day, I'll be in pretty good shape.

After a quick dinner at Shoney's, I returned to my room, re-spooled my reels, and did my tackle.

JANUARY 23rd

Second day of competition. We ran to the Dead River first thing this morning. It warmed up a little and had some overcast. They are predicting some storms this afternoon, some of them pretty heavy. We started in the canal at Dead River where I was the second boat in. We fished it quite thoroughly for about 45 minutes before my partner landed his only keeper of the day on a little black-and-chartreuse ringworm. The fish hit in about 2 feet of water right off of the edge of the grassline. The canal is about 12 or 14 feet deep. I was fishing at the vegetation line out into the deeper water thinking that maybe the fish were holding out away from shore. I wasn't really sure, but his first fish came very shallow.

As I eased out of that branch of the canal, I noticed several other boats, mostly the same boats that I had seen in there the day before. I basically fished back and forth with them for several hours without a bite. I never saw anyone land a fish. Rick Clunn came fishing through using a Slug-Go type bait very fast and said he hadn't caught one. The wind was picking up and I really believed that staying in the canals was the best thing to do the rest of the day.

I left that canal at approximately 10:30 a.m. and went to another canal system where I ran into Ken Cook, who was obviously guarding that canal as best he could. I kind of eased in with him and fished it until about 12:30 p.m. without a strike (and as far as I know he didn't land one either). This was the canal where my partner had caught one in the day before. It was only about 12:30 and I wasn't panicking, but I was getting kind of concerned of the fact that I hadn't had a bite yet. Even though it's tough, you still have to catch a couple a day.

So I pulled out of that canal and went around into the Dora canal, which looks on the map exactly the same as the other canal we fished in all morning. Several boats were in there, but the traffic wasn't too heavy, so we began fishing. About that time we had a massive storm develop. For a few minutes there I thought we were going to see a funnel cloud drop out of the sky — it was really bad with torrential rain and winds. You could hardly see your hand in front of your face.

Obviously, I wasn't able to feel my worm at this time, so I picked up a spinnerbait rod I had on the deck (a big gold-bladed 1/2-ounce spinnerbait) and I made my first cast in that downpour against a patch of lily pads. I caught my only keeper of the day. The rain only lasted 30 minutes and I threw the spinnerbait the entire time without getting another strike. I went back to the worm and finished out the day, managing to only catch one crappie.

That was it. I ran to the weigh-in, pushed it to the limit and barely got in on time. My one fish weighed 13 ounces. So for two days I've got 3 pounds, 3 ounces. The cutoff for cashing a check is 4 1/2 pounds, so a couple of nice fish is all I need to really move up. Obviously big fish aren't being caught — the biggest fish of the tournament today was 3 pounds, 3 ounces.

After talking with my partner for tomorrow, I'm not really comfortable with the situation. As luck would have it, I drew this guy in the MegaBucks tournament last year. In that tournament, he agreed to do what I wanted to do — which was to go for broke and try and catch a big one.

We're about in the same boat weight-wise. He just explained to me that he wants to go to Lake Dora tomorrow for at least half the day, which doesn't thrill me. I had fished Dora so thoroughly the third day of practice and everyone I talked to that went to Dora has not had a bite. So it seems like a very risky

situation. Dora is noted for its big fish, but there is a big possibility that I could blank tomorrow. I just don't think it is a good move, but then I have to respect the fact that he did what I wanted to do last year at MegaBucks.

We are going to use my boat. He said we could do what I want to do the second half of the day, but once you're in Dora, you're committed. I put away all of my light line and light worms that I had been using and spooled up with some 20- and 25-pound line on two flipping sticks for tomorrow (one with a light weight and one with a heavy weight). I guess we'll just go to Dora and flip all day. If I could get just one good bite, I know it would be worth a paycheck.

JANUARY 24th

Final day of competition. My partner remains dead set on going to Lake Dora and spending at least half of a day. He said he caught a 6-pounder and a 4-pounder in there the first day of practice. He is the only guy I know who has caught anything out of Dora this week. I feel kind of obligated to ride with him. You've got to understand this is a super-nice guy, a real good Christian guy, who reeks of confidence almost to a point of excess. He is so vocal and so sure that we're going to catch fish today in Dora. Let's face it man, I spent a whole day of practice in Dora and never had a bite, so it's really hard for me to be optimistic. But I do know the quality of the fish that are in Dora so I keep trying to think positively.

We are one of the first boats in Dora — as a matter of fact, we are probably the only boat in Dora. I saw maybe one other boat in

Dora all the rest of the day. We had overcast skies and rapidly falling temperatures (it was getting pretty cold) with high winds. The wind made it difficult to flip the reeds. I would go back and forth between a 1/4-ounce and a 3/8-ounce weight. Most of the time I ended up using a 3/8-ounce because of the heavy wind early in the day. We fished some very good areas, where he said he had caught fish. And I believed him. I know the kind of fish the area can produce.

And I tried to do what I was supposed to do — envision a bass under every reed and every possible ambush point. I played that game all day long. I literally flipped every good-looking stretch of cover (reeds particularly) there is in Dora for 8 1/2 hours. I flipped every possible reed in the lake that had some kind of water under it. And I never had a strike.

I had resigned myself to the fact that if I didn't leave Dora by 2:35 or 2:40 p.m. (since my check-in time was 3:10) that I wouldn't make it back in time for weigh-in. At 2:39 , I got my first and only strike of the day — and it was a pretty awesome strike. I flipped into a clump of maidencane with a couple of reeds in it and the whole patch shook. Feeling the strike, I tightened up, set the hook and it felt like the fish I needed — about a 4-pounder or bigger. But then that problem with execution that has plagued me too many times this season made an appearance.

I may have given the fish a little too much time. A lot of times on those visual strikes — when you see the reeds shake — you set the hook too soon. I wanted to make sure the fish had the bait. When I dropped my rod to check if the fish had the bait, I gave him a little too much time and he swam out the backside of the reed clump. When I set the hook, the line was around the patch of reeds. The fish thrashed and jumped around while I was doing everything I could to get him past the reed clump. I managed to get him up to the reed clump, but before I could reach him, he pulled free.

Literally it was my last flip of the day and I wish I would have never gotten that bite. It was probably one of the most discouraging things of the season. You work your butt off all day long to get one bite and then blow it. It's not that bad when you fish hard and don't get a strike, there's nothing you can do about that. But when you screw up, it's a cardinal sin, especially when that was a fish that would have put me well into the money. That was probably a $1,500 or $1,600 fish.

As I was idling through the Dead River canal, I just wanted to shoot myself. I just couldn't believe it had happened. On my way across Eustis, I ran into another competitor, Gerald Smith, who was broken down with a spun prop hub. I knew that my partner and I didn't have any fish anyway, so I offered to take him in. Instead, he asked us to tow him over to the shoreline where we helped him change his prop out. We followed him in to make sure he got in.

That was the end of the story. There is nothing worse than coming in front of 3,000 people with zero fish. It was a standing-room-only crowd and some of my friends and relatives were in town, which added insult to

injury. I would so much have loved to have caught that big bass, raced back to the weigh-in, totalled 7 1/2 pounds, made the money and been a happy camper. But that's not the way it is. Instead, I get zero money. I fall farther behind and it's not real good for my confidence. I'm pretty miserable right now, to be honest with you.

JANUARY 25th

By now we've gone to Disney World, Epcot Center and Sea World and I'm not doing a very good job of putting this behind me. I've been hard to live with for the past two days. Diane says she's sick of it. But she's dealing with it pretty good. I'm just not dealing with this whole thing well. I keep reflecting back on the stupid mistakes, missed opportunities and missed fish and bad decisions.

I think I've got 15 pounds for three invitational tournaments, which would have been unimaginable until now. I've never gone through a stretch of six tournaments without finishing in the money. Consistency has always been my strong suit.

I would almost have to go out and try to do this poorly. A lot of the problem is I have tried to hit a home run too many times. I'm trying to make things happen instead of letting them happen. And this kind of slump breeds indecisiveness. I'm not fishing like myself and I'm letting it bother me worse than ever. As much as I try not to let it bother me, and I try to be optimistic, I'm not dealing with it well.

And I keep having this nagging thought, "this is when I need to be doing my best." I'm doing this book and I've got a baby coming. I need to be doing my best; but I'm doing my worst. After nine years, you would think I would get progressively better, not faltering like I'm doing. I could see one tournament or two, but not six in a row. This is ridiculous.

Chapter 10

The End
Of a Dry Spell

Florida Bassmaster Top 100
February 19-22, 1992
St. Johns River

FEBRUARY 15th

Arrived in Palatka today with just a brief pause in my schedule before practice for the Bassmaster Top 100 Tournament that begins tomorrow on the St. Johns River. Things have been so hectic, that I'm looking forward to getting back on the water.

Yesterday, I spoke at a St. Louis sport show, finishing up at about 10 p.m. eastern time. I drove through the night to reach Cincinnati at three in the morning. I dropped Diane off at the house, dropped some of my bags and picked up new bags that I already had packed. My boat was ready. Two friends, Mike Duncan who's an amateur from Cincinnati that's going to fish in the tournament, and George Richie, just a good friend of mine from my old bass club days, are going to help with the long drive to Florida.

I slept all the way to the Florida border. I was a tired son of a gun. I've been doing shows almost every day. About 10 cities in the last 15 days. So many cities that I managed to even get on the wrong plane in one city. I ended up in Charlotte, N.C., when I should have been in Charleston, S.C. Or maybe it was the other way around.

We spent the night with my friend Bo Boren at his house in Palatka.

FEBRUARY 16th

First day of practice. The weather was beautiful fishing-wise, with 70-degree temperatures and a little breeze and cloud cover all day. It drizzled a little bit. It's the kind of weather where we should have just ripped their heads off.

Today, George and I fished the first three hours of morning on a low incoming tide right in the St. Johns River near the housing headquarters (the Holiday Inn in Palatka). Most of the hydrilla I remembered is dead or gone. There is a lot of mucky bottom where the hydrilla used to be. That's an indication that the vegetation has decayed and gone to the bottom.

The water temperature is right, but we only managed to catch one small bass and a couple of gar there. At about 10:30 a.m., I ran down the river and locked into Rodman Reservoir. The water is extremely low in Rodman (it is being drawn down by state officials for habitat enhancement), but there were a ton of tournament boats and local fishermen in there. And a lot of shiner fishermen catching some big fish. I stuck mainly with the Slug-Go in the very clear water with scattered hydrilla and lots of stumps. I concentrated on big stump flats on both the east and west sides of the Rodman canal.

The water averaged 7 feet deep in the east side and 4 feet on the west. I started in the morning on the west. It was very cloudy and we managed to catch several pickerel and three keeper bass.

It was not as good as I would have imagined. By the time I got to the deep side near the dam, the sun had come out and you could see bottom. The water was gin clear. Then the wind laid down and we weren't able to catch anything. I don't think this tournament can be won in Rodman from what I've seen. But I would have liked to have fished that east side under optimum conditions.

Maybe Lake George is happening. We plan on trailering to Lake George in the morning. The bass should be spawning there. The water temperature is right. The moon is full. But I've not seen any beds in Rodman to speak of.

We ate tonight at Golden Corral, which is the place to eat in Palatka. The most food for the money. It's about 9:30. After going over my maps a little bit, I'm going to bed.

FEBRUARY 17th

Second day of practice. A very frustrating day. Perfect conditions. Overcast, breezy, air temperature in the 70s. Tailor-made fishing conditions I would think. But the fish just aren't biting.

Got up about 5:30 and we drove all the way down to Welatka at the mouth of the St. Johns River and put our boat in at a fish camp there. We bought a map of Lake George. We were in the water right at daylight.

We began working the western shoreline of the lake where Juniper, Salt Springs and Silver Glen Springs, all come in. The water is very clear at the mouth of the springs. Lots of grass and lots of old beds. And there are a lot of local fishermen, just hundreds sitting out there dunking shiners on these old bedding areas. I cruised through them, fishing a Rattlin' Rogue and a Kalin Hop-a-Long (hard and soft versions of jerkbaits) over the top of the beds. I was trying to see the beds and I just couldn't see any fish on the beds. Maybe it's my eyes. I'm wearing some really good Hobie sunglasses and paying attention to what's in the water.

I'm just not able to see very many fish, which may be attributable to the fact that we have overcast conditions. The fish I've seen aren't very big. I haven't gone into the springs and I won't. That's not my kind of fishing. It's gin-clear. It's sight-fishing with tubejigs. It's just not my thing. I'm trying to find fish that are moving up to spawn or moving out after the spawn. I fished intensely outside the grassline. You would think the fish that are outside the grassline would be staging, intending to move in to spawn in these areas. So I tried a Rat-L-Trap, spinnerbait and even swam a worm.

The box score was one non-keeper at the end of the day. With the perfect conditions, I just can't understand it.

I spoke with several anglers on the water, which doesn't usually happen unless the fishing is extremely tough. Everyone I talked to on Lake George — Randy Blaukat, Danny Correia, Larry Nixon, Johnny Borden — had not caught a keeper bass.

It just doesn't make any sense to me. The moon is right, the water temperature is right. This was my best bet. I really think that Lake George is more suited to my style of fishing, but it's just not happening.

I pulled out at about 3:30 p.m. and trailered across to Crescent Lake. I fished a couple of shell beds over in Crescent, but didn't catch any fish. We got blown off in the last 30 minutes of daylight by a tremendous storm. It came across with winds of 50 m.p.h., heavy rain and lightning. Luckily I saw it coming and we sprinted for the boat dock.

We rode out the storm at Hardee's and then headed to registration at the Holiday Inn in Palatka. We're back at the room and getting ready to turn in again. I'm really unsure of what I should do tomorrow. I believe I'm going to fish north. I'm going to fish the spawning canals north of Palatka.

FEBRUARY 18th

Final day of practice. Same conditions. Almost a carbon copy of yesterday. I can't remember coming to Florida for this many days and having overcast and balmy conditions. Maybe the lack of sun is why the fish aren't coming up on the nest.

The clouds should really be conducive to the fish being active. I fished the main river up to where Hank Parker supposedly won the Super B.A.S.S. years ago. I divided my day between fishing main river eelgrass and docks and the other half of the day fishing canals. There aren't a whole lot of canals. I've kind of moved back and forth between the two patterns. I managed to catch two keeper fish in the main river at the mouth of a canal in the eelgrass. That was just about it.

In the canals, I could see a few old beds but nothing fresh. I did a lot of flipping with a 1/2- and 3/4-ounce weight around matted hyacinths and duckweed on the side of the canals.

I caught one bass in a canal on a gold Rattlin' Rogue. But I never had another strike in another two hours. It almost seems like a fluke.

I just don't understand it. The only place that I've caught any fish at all is Rodman. From the talk around the tournament, maybe that's the place to go. All the guys say that they can't catch them anywhere else, so they're going to Rodman. I don't know how much pressure Rodman can take. But it's a big lake. The forecast is for a breezy overcast day again tomorrow. If it is, Rodman's probably the place to go.

At the pairings meeting tonight, I drew a nice man from Texas as my amateur partner. He'll ride with me to Rodman.

We ordered a pizza to save some time and worked on my tackle. My friend George was very helpful with my tackle. He helped strip my reels. It's nice to have somebody with you. I called my wife and took care of a little business. I've had several calls from sponsors and sports shows. All part of the business of being a bass pro.

FEBRUARY 19th

First day of competition. Wonder how suicide would play in this book. We might sell more copies if I killed myself here at the seventh tournament of the year? It's really not funny. I caught a whoping total of a pound and 12 ounces today. I've just completely blown myself out of this tournament.

The St. Johns River remains a great fishery, particularly in the Rodman pool.

In the fourth flight, I ran to Rodman. Fortunately, my arrival met the lock schedule just right. I cut every corner and just barely made it into the locks as the doors were closing. Fifty-seven boats locked through to Rodman today. That told me something was happening in Rodman. There were some tremendous stringers caught in there today. Pete Thliveros had 25 pounds, Shaw Grigsby had over 20 and Rob Kilby had over 20. Denny Brauer had over 20. Chet Douthit had 18. Randy Blaukat had 15. And that was just the beginning.

I must have fished Rodman with a bag over my head or my hands tied because I caught a pair of 14-ounce bass. I really don't understand it. I fished those timber plots with a gold Bomber Long A jerkbait and a spinnerbait. Maybe I just didn't get the right area. There's something I obviously didn't do right.

The conditions were still favorable. The fish should have been eating that Long A and that spinnerbait. But I couldn't get them to bite it. I'm not sure what I'm going to do tomorrow. I've got three days left. The only thing that I do know is that I need to pick a different area. It's such a huge area out there in those trees. You make the right drift and you catch 15 pounds. You make the wrong drift through them and you catch 2 pounds like I did. The only problem is that sunny skies for tomorrow. If that happens, I'm pretty much out of this thing.

I'm not going to win this one, that's for doggone sure. I'd have to have a miracle just to make a paycheck as it is now.

I did a little bit of tackle and watched the Winter Olympics for a while. We're getting ready to go to bed. It's 9 o'clock.

FEBRUARY 20th

Second day of competition. I went to Rodman again today. Short day over there, though. I didn't get to fish very long. Because the way the locks are scheduled, and being in the first flight, I was only able to spend about four and a half hours in there.

It was breezy and a little overcast early before getting bright and sunny and tough later on. I drifted more through the center of the east stump field today. A lot of boats out there. Today I could see the bottom because it wasn't windy. A lot of the guys that finished pretty high yesterday are here, so I basically tried to stay away from them. I'd make my drifts away from everybody else. But it is a huge area.

I never fired my big motor up other than to go into this area. I caught seven squeakers there today that weighed 7 pounds, 7 ounces. At least it was a limit.

I didn't get to cull and my partner only caught one (a 3 1/2

**Bass like this one, caught fun fishing before
the St. Johns tournament, come all too seldom.**

pounder). Can you imagine, he catches one and I catch seven? Yet, his one a 3 1/2-pounder, and all of mine are 1-pound fish.

Those little fish seemed to like that silver Long A when you've got it in the right place. I caught a couple in one little area as I circled it several times. Tomorrow I just plan on doing the same doggone thing. I'll just go to Rodman and play the weather and pick my area.

I've only got less than 10 pounds so I'm pretty much out of this thing unless a miracle happens. I'm pretty much out of everything. My mom called me tonight. I guess she's trying to boost me up. She knows I'm really hurting and things are going bad. But I guess in retrospect everything else is good in my life. I got a lot of good things happening. A good home life and I'm making plenty of money off of the sponsors and the shows.

It's a real lucrative time in my career right now, but the bottom line is I'm a tournament fisherman and performance in these tournaments is what I thrive on. I let my life and my feelings be dictated by how I'm doing in the tournaments. I just need a good one. Maybe tomorrow.

FEBRUARY 21st

Third day of competition. I finally caught some decent fish today. Maybe I figured something out for tomorrow. About 70 boats locked through to Rodman. The conditions were good — cloudy, breezy, overcast. Nothing real heavy, just good Rodman fishing conditions for that clear water. I can't ever recall this many days in Florida when it was being cloudy and overcast.

Today I took a different line again through that big timber flat on the east side of Rodman. I stayed closer to the south shoreline this time, actually fishing down towards the concrete dam. There is a lot more hydrilla in 4 or 5 feet of water. I caught my first bass today between the stumps with a gold Rouge.

The cloud cover and windy conditions made the gold Rouge a better choice than the silver Long A. I thought maybe that rattle in the Rogue would make a difference. So I went to the Rogue with a shallow bill, fishing it on a 6 1/2-foot medium-action All Star rod, and 10-pound test line to get it to reach a depth of 4 feet. The first bass I caught kind of tuned me into something.

I was jerking the Rogue a couple feet under the surface in a rhythmic cadence. When I paused to negotiate a stump with my trolling motor, I stopped my retrieve just for a second. A Rouge, with its neutral buoyancy, kind of suspends at any level. At that point, a 3-pounder just about ripped the rod out of my hands. It may have been a fluke, but I wasn't taking any chances. I began to fan-cast between the stumps and between the trees, concentrating on the hydrilla more than the stumps.

I made it a point to stop the lure at least one time for a second or two during every retrieve. And I proceeded to kick their tails. I caught 16 keepers and culled up to a 12-pound, 14-ounce stringer. And I didn't lose a bass.

I'm using Gamakatsu hooks on my Rogue, that are very sharp. I was able to land even the bass that were lightly hooked in the gills or outside the face. My partner was nice enough to help me land one of my bigger ones, about a 3 1/4-pounder.

It was just a good day. The boats around me aren't catching fish. That's the strange part. I basically culled all day long. Every time I would leave that general area, I would quit getting bites. So obviously that area right around the dam in Rodman is a happening place.

This moved me up some. I've got about 21 pounds now. Another good limit — 13 pounds or more — might slide me into a paycheck. That would do a lot for my morale, I guarantee you. Another quick meal with Ken Cook and Greg Hines and off to bed.

FEBRUARY 22nd

Final day of competition. I finally caught fish on two straight days. And it feels real good. I returned to the same area in Rodman and the results were great. Fishing that scattered hydrilla, the day started off with a bang. Using that stop-and-go retrieve with the gold Rogue, I caught a 3-pounder and 2 1/2 in the first 15 minutes. It went sporadic throughout the day.

It got kind of slow during the middle of the day and then I hit another flurry at the end. I ended up catching about 15 keepers today. I only lost one fish — a 2-pounder. It may have cost me a couple of places.

I ended up catching 13 pounds, 13 ounces, which was enough to give me 35-5 total weight and put me in the money. I finished 23rd and won $3,000. This marks the end of a long dry spell. It feels great. I felt like I had a rhythm down. I was fishing good again.

It was just like the old days. It felt great. George

Winning Ways

This tournament turned out to be a battle of the sight-fishermen. The top finishers fished finesse baits for spawn and pre-spawn bass in Rodman Reservoir, which was enduring a man-made drawdown. Hometown favorite Pete Thliveros caught 69 pounds, 7 ounces of bass by using a smoke-blue colored G-4 tubejig rigged with 1/8- and 1/16-ounce sinkers, a 1/0 Shaw Grigsby's High Performance Hook and 12-pound line. He targeted a spawning flat in Rodman that features an 8-foot creek channel that snakes through the area. The combination of shallow spawning grounds and adjacent deep water held plenty of spawners. Thliveros also caught bass in the area on a topwater plug in the same area and a Carolina-rigged grub in the main river channel.

and Mike are going to help me drive on home, where I'll get to spend one day. I'll take care of phone calls, re-pack and deposit this check.

I am 16 pounds out of the Classic in the Top 100 standings. Despite the lousy year I've had, if I would have had a good first day at Lanier and caught a little 8- or 9-pound bag (I caught a pound), and would have caught a similar weight the first day here at St. Johns, I would have been right in the Classic chase.

It's really sad how a couple of days can screw your whole year up. But we've got a lot of invitationals left, big-weight tournaments, and I feel good about it again. I feel good about myself again.

The ups and downs of professional bass fishing. It's 10:30 p.m. and we've got 600 miles ahead of us.

Chapter 11

On a Roll — Finally!

Texas Bassmaster Invitational
March 18-20, 1992
Sam Rayburn Reservoir

MARCH 14th

Sam Rayburn Reservoir in the middle of east Texas.

Diane and I are doing the little things to get ready for tomorrow's first practice day. She is about six months pregnant and a lot of my thoughts find their way to the baby. I haven't even been able to attend the first two natural childbirth classes with her, but she understands. She's very healthy and things are going good. We just got a sonogram done and found out it looks like it's going to be a boy. At least that's what they think it's going to be.

Financially, mentally, and overall I'm pretty comfortable. Things are going pretty good. It really helped to make the money in the last tournament. Hopefully I'm just going to start a string of good finishes and maybe pull off one of those miracles. I know Rayburn is a place where we can catch a whole bunch of fish and that I could maybe make up 15 or 20 pounds realistically.

Sam Rayburn is about 10 feet above normal and all of the launch ramps except one are underwater. That should make things interesting.

My game plan for the first day is to go back into the trees as far as I can possibly drag my boat. I fished here last year and the water was 4 feet high. I got back in the trees and caught quite a few fish. The water is now 66 degrees and the full moon is coming up. The fish have got to be preparing to spawn.

I probably will throw a spinnerbait a lot tomorrow and swim a weightless lizard around the pine trees in the Black Forest area. I really believe that that's as good an area as there is. I'll probably end up spending most of my time there in this tournament. There is a lot of grass on the outside if I choose to fish grass or need to resort to it.

I will be fishing by myself. Diane can't fish with me anymore because the water is too rough on her stomach.

This afternoon I shot a commercial for Reel Craw, the fish scent that I'm associated with. It was with Tommy Martin, Larry Nixon, Guido Hibdon, Harold Allen, and two new team members, Kevin VanDam and Zell Rowland. That took a couple of hours. Then I came back and started working on my tackle. I'm going to try to get in bed as early as I can.

MARCH 15th

First day of practice and it was a pretty rough one. We had a high pressure system move through. The clouds kind of cleared out last night and it got really bright and sunny. Boy, the fish just didn't bite very good. I fished some areas back in the timber where the water is very high. It's really hard to get back into the shallow timber, but I fished back in some places that I almost couldn't get out of.

I caught several little bass, but not very many keepers. I did hook a pretty good fish on a bush in about 4 or 5 feet of water by flipping a pumpkinseed jig. But the spinnerbait bite I anticipated never happened.

Tomorrow I plan on spending the whole day in the hydrilla. My house mate, Fish Fishburne, and I are kind of working together on this deal. He also fished back in the flooded timber and didn't do too well.

The water is falling probably 6 inches a day. That may account for the fact that the fish weren't real shallow (1- to 2-foot range).

Tonight was nice. Diane had dinner ready when we came off the water before we had to leave for registration. At registration I got to meet and talk to my new boss at Zebco, Gary Dollahon. I got some of the new Zebco Pro reels and the new EX Series reels and they look really nice. I'm going to try a couple of them out tomorrow.

It's about 9:15 p.m. right now. Hopefully we'll be in bed before 10 and I can get seven or eight hours of sleep.

MARCH 16th

Second practice day. This lake is killing me. With the water up 10 feet, the inside grassline is in 13 or 14 feet of water. I would imagine that these fish are somewhere between the hydrilla line and the shoreline. The problem is with the water being so high I'm really having difficulty — even with my Lowrance X-60 — staying on the edge of the grassline.

I really believe the fish are on the bare spots just inside the grass. I spent all day on outside grass and just got a handful of bites and only a couple of keepers. I should have caught more quality fish considering the amount of prime water I fished today. The wind hampered me a little bit in the afternoon, making it more difficult to stay right on the grasslines. And the grasslines on this lake twist and turn. I have to rely on the contour of the bank and my electronics. Not knowing the little hot spots, I'm really struggling here. I wasn't able to catch them inside at all and I'm not catching them very good outside.

This lake has got so many fish in it. Surely some people are catching them good.

I primarily used a Carolina-rigged lizard and deep-cranked with a Mann's 20+ crankbait on the inside edge of the grasslines. It was fairly unsuccessful.

I pulled off the water right about dark in time to attend a barbecue staged by Skeeter Boats and Stanley Jigs. It was a nice function, but coming back from the town of Jasper, I'm physically exhausted. Just need a good night's sleep and try to figure out what I'm going to do tomorrow.

It's supposed to be cloudy and rainy. If they don't bite tomorrow with those conditions, there's something wrong. I'm going to spend the first half a day back inside the timber and see what happens.

MARCH 17th

Final day of practice. Got up at daylight and was deathly ill. Maybe it was something I ate at that darn barbecue last night, but I've got major stomach pains. I stayed in bed until about 7:15 a.m. I finally just said to heck with it and I went out anyway. It was pretty miserable the first half of the day until I got whatever it was out of my system. I know a lot of people have been having the stomach flu — maybe I've got a touch of that.

Despite the awful start, today was a brighter day for me on the water. It was 70 degrees, overcast, light winds from the southwest. Just a good day for fishing. But by noon, the spinnerbait and plastic lizard had only produced a couple of keepers back in the timber. I just haven't been able to find an area where I feel like there are a lot of fish.

In the afternoon, I began fishing buck bushes in 4 feet of water outside of the hardwood trees. I really think that's where a lot of these fish are. However, I just haven't been able to really home in on them. I ran into Zell Rowland on the water. Zell and I have become pretty good friends since doing a lot of seminars together. Zell said that he was hammering them back in the timber that I've been fishing on a small (1/4-ounce) spinnerbait. He suggested that I drop down my spinnerbait size.

This was about one o'clock today. I was fairly close to Twin Dikes Marina and another area where I've caught fish in the past. I moved back inside hardwood trees where the wind was making a pretty good ripple on the water. I caught five or six keepers (including a 7-pounder) in a 150-yard stretch. I could see several spawning beds on the bottom of what looked like an old road bed that wound through the trees. That obviously was a key feature. I believe the fish are moving up the road beds to spawn because they are clear of debris and get direct sunlight. That's my guess anyway.

The most effective lure is a 1/4-ounce white spinnerbait with a No. 4 nickel blade.

Trying to duplicate the pattern elsewhere, I moved out and flipped a few bushes in the same general area. The results were spotty, at best. At least I have one area that I have confidence in. The problem is if the wind blows from the south (as predicted), I could be in trouble because it's a fairly open area. It's on the end of a big point leading into a cove. I'll just have to see what happens.

My partner draw is a nice guy from Minnesota, who is hearing-impaired. He said he has been catching a lot of fish on a topwater bait in two particular pockets (close to where I caught my fish) that are on sheltered banks out of the wind. So that's an option if the wind blows. We're going to use my boat and just kind of do my thing in the morning and his in the afternoon unless the wind won't let us get on my area.

The forecast tomorrow is for high winds and for rain, so they should bite the spinnerbait tomorrow like they did today. I feel a lot more confident than I did. I plan on spooling some fairly heavy line (17- or 20-pound) on that spinnerbait to combat the timber.

The alarm is set for 5:30 a.m.

Despite the high water, there were plenty of big bass surrendered by big Sam Rayburn.

MARCH 18th

First day of competition. What a day. I caught them fairly ewll, but I was really fortunate. I had a few little problems today. I noticed the wind was blowing heavily from the south and probably blowing way too hard on my area. There were 3- and 4-foot waves. Steve's area, however, was sheltered. In his area, we started with a Zara Spook early. There was a lot of fishing pressure in the area. I managed to hook and lose my first fish of the day, which managed to get a pine tree between me and him. It was a 4- to 5-pound fish. It just didn't start my day off right.

We proceeded on to a couple more pockets and Steve caught two keepers on a small spinnerbait. I managed to catch one keeper at about 9:15 a.m. by pitching the bait back into the trees and winding it out through the cover very slowly. The water is fairly stained, with a visibility of less than 2 feet.

At about 11:30 a.m., I started to noticed that my trolling motor batteries didn't have the power they should have. I checked all of my connections and everything seemed fine. But I just didn't have any juice. I didn't know if I had a dead cell in my battery or what.

Without much trolling motor power, I moved into a sheltered cove with flooded shoreline grass. I began throwing my spinnerbait and soon caught a fish about 2 1/4 pounds (my second fish of the day). Another sheltered pocket surrendered a 14-inch bass to my spinnerbait.

At that point, we wheeled into the weigh-in area and borrowed a battery from B.A.S.S. assistant tournament director Tripp Wheldon.

By this time, the wind had let up enough to allow me to fish my primary area and we immediately proceeded there for the last three hours of the day. The wind looked just right when I got in there. The water wasn't too muddy. Steve immediately caught a 2 1/4-pound bass. A well-placed cast with the spinnerbait between two pine trees on the bank where I had caught a keeper the other day produced an enormous boil in the water. A fish knocked slack in my line, but when I set the hook there was nothing there. He missed the bait completely, which is typical of a spawning fish. I made several casts back into the same spot trying to get the fish to bite, without success.

It was then that I discovered a bunch of vines wrapped around my trolling motor. As I stopped to tear the vines loose, Steve, who had given me plenty of opportunity to catch that fish, did just that on a larger spinnerbait that landed between the same two pines. I lipped a 5 1/2-pound bass for him.

That was kind of disheartening, knowing that if that fish would have just had a little bit better eyesight, I would have caught that

Young Kevin VanDam rolled at Rayburn with five bass weighing 31 pounds, 11 ounces.

son of a gun. The same bank produced three small fish for me and four for Steve. One of my fish was a 6 1/2-pounder that I quickly subdued. I basically just leaned hard and swung the fish right in the boat. She never knew she was hooked. She did all of her fighting on the floor of the boat. That made my day. It was a gift fish.

After that we caught only non-keepers until 10 minutes before the weigh in when I moved out to some bushes in 3 feet of water and began flipping a pumpkinseed jig. It was there that I caught my fifth fish, barely a keeper, giving me a total of 11 pounds 15 ounces for the day.

That puts me in 61st place, just barely in the money.

We're on our way back from Wal-mart right now. We exchanged a battery. It's just been a long day. We're really tired. We ate at Charlie's Barbecue in Jasper, which is owned by the parents of Fish's ex-girlfriend. I didn't eat any barbecue, though.

MARCH 19th

Second day of competition. My partner and I decided to fish my area first. The forecast calls for sunny skies and extremely heavy winds today. They produced some huge waves. After that boat ride, my back will never be the same. I arrived to find my area flat, calm and sunny. My area was protected from the strong north wind.

The bass didn't bite my spinnerbait, as I had anticipated. However, my partner caught a keeper by flipping a 6-inch plastic lizard into the buck bushes in the backs of little pockets — which had been his pattern throughout the week.

With that success in mind, we ran north to his area, a set of pockets near Veach Basin, which took nearly 45 minutes in the rough water. My partner caught two more solid keepers before my trolling motor quit. I began checking circuit breakers

and all terminal connections. Everything looked fine. So I pulled my spare trolling motor out of the rod locker, I wired it in, but it didn't work.

One of my switches looked a little melted, so I realized that I was probably saddled with a burnt switch. I had a spare of everything else, but I didn't have a spare switch with me. So we were basically dead in the water at 10 a.m. Our only alternative was to make the long, hard run back to the service yard to get it repaired by the MotorGuide service crew.

The 45-minute run was just gut-pounding. I pushed it pretty hard, because obviously I was pretty wound up. When I arrived, the service crew was not around, so I retrieved a spare switch and test light from my vehicle. It was about noon when we found and corrected the problem.

With a working trolling motor, we left at 12:30 p.m — leaving us just two and a half hours to fish. I didn't have a single fish. I didn't have the time to make the run all the way back to my partner's water, so we decided to go back to my little area (which is within 10 minutes of the marina) and flip that 6-inch lizard in bushes in 4 to 5 feet of water.

My partner immediately boated a non-keeper and then lost a decent bass. I soon followed his lead with my first keeper, a 14 1/2-incher. About 10 minutes later, I caught my second keeper, followed by one about 5 1/2 pounds. Then I ended up catching one more fish of 2 1/2 pounds or so. That gave me 10 pounds for the day.

I lost two fish down deep in the bushes, which kept me from limiting out. But I'm not complaining. I'm thrilled with my catch considering all of the mechanical problems I encountered. And I'm in 45th place.

Tomorrow my partner will be Pete Thliveros, who had 18 or 19 pounds today, including one fish that weighed almost 10 pounds. He's Caro-

Winning Ways

Florida pro Shaw Grigsby won his third B.A.S.S. event on Sam Rayburn, but, for the first time, his pattern didn't involve a tubejig and sight-fishing. Grigsby's 62 1/2 pounds came on a week when record rainfall had the reservoir level 10 feet above normal. Grigsby showed his resourcefulness by changing tactics throughout the three days of competition. He started by bed-fishing with a Guido Bug on 25-pound test line. The next two days, he caught bass by cranking and Carolina-rigging a plastic lizard around the base of trees and vegetation in 5 feet of water.

lina-rigging the outside grass and he's adamant about doing it again tomorrow. He's ahead of me in total weight, so I agree.

Still in a good mood. I just finished working on my tackle and Diane has fixed a real nice dinner of chicken and rice. We're going to pull the boat out here in just a few minutes and pack everything up. At this point in her pregnancy, Diane can't really carry things, so I'm going to help her pack tonight and it will probably be one of those late nights.

MARCH 20th

Final day of competition. Well, we're on our way home. It's about 10 o'clock at night. I had a little less eventful day today, but I did manage to make the money. I finished in 48th place with a total weight of 30 pounds, 15 ounces. I made the money by 3 ounces. I can't tell you how good it feels to make a check in two tournaments in a row.

My score today was five bass weighing 9 pounds. I just did not have one of those big son of a guns jump on my line today like I did the other two days. That would have made the difference.

Pete and I Carolina-rigged in the deep (13 to 14 feet) grass most of the day, but they just didn't bite well out there. I caught three fish and he had two small keepers.

We did go to my stretches of bushes with about two hours left, where we both managed to finish off our limit by flipping a lizard (which was yesterday's pattern). I caught a 2 1/4-pounder with just a few minutes remaining to cull a small fish and sneak into the top 50 money-paying positions.

The tournament was won by Shaw Grigsby with 62 pounds, who targeted mostly spawning bass on roadbeds. My roommate, Fish Fishburne, ended up in sixth place by catching spawners the last two days. Obviously, if you were real good at that spawn fishing, that was the way to catch the big ones.

At least I'm in the money and I'm back on track. It helps my mental attitude.

Chapter 12

The Business Side Of Tournament Fishing

The little-discussed aspect of the sport

Two big-name pros, Rick Clunn and Larry Nixon, passed the million-dollar mark in career earnings in recent years. Both are recognized as outstanding fishermen and tournament competitors.

But what may have been overshadowed is the fact that these anglers and others have made nearly as much money — if not more — through the business side of fishing, including endorsement contracts, public appearances and other fishing-related business ventures.

Although the fan adulation and the actual time spent on the water have an almost romantic appeal to it for the weekend angler/ aspiring bass pro, understanding the business side of this sport is the key to making a good, lucrative living — from catching these little green fish. There is so much more involved than just catching fish.

I don't profess to know everything there is about the business of fishing, but I am more than happy to share what I have learned over the years through these pages. At the very least, it will give the fishing fan an inside look at what goes on off-of-the-water. And it may provide some ambitious young pro enough information to make the financial side of fishing a little easier to comprehend.

I've been fortunate enough to have had insights into the business side of fishing shared with me by other pros. And I have some college education. I've also been able to surround myself with a support team that has areas of expertise that I do not.

I had enough college that I really don't ever feel inadequate in the business part of the fishing world right now. I guess when my sponsors start talking about price points and S.K.U.s (Stock Keeping Units) and things like that I've kind of educated myself to contribute to that discussion. As far as contract negotiations and things, I've had to stumble around a little bit, but it didn't take a long time to pick up on it.

It's more important to have a good tax accountant or tax lawyer than anything else. I have a good tax accountant, a lady that worked for the IRS for about 15 years, which gives her a behind-the-scenes-understanding. She has grown up with my career. So she understands it inside and out. I think that's very important. She's probably the only accountant in Cincinnati who's ever handled a professional bass angler.

She saw a career that was making $20,000 to $30,000 a year go to a career that made $200,000 one year. In my biggest year, 1990, when I won the All American, she certainly earned her money.

I would recommend having an attorney. It's just a good safeguard. Personally, I have never needed a lawyer. My contracts are very straight-forward and simple. But I don't have the big Team Brunswick-type long-term contracts that can be worth six figures or more a year, and have many clauses and stipulations.

My contracts are pretty simple. I draft up about 50 percent of my own contracts. Some of the contracts in this business seem complex, at first, but if you read it a couple of times, you can figure it out pretty well. Most are basic and straight-forward. You'll find in the fishing business that just about all the contracts say the same basic thing.

One major consideration with any endorsement contract is an "out clause." An out clause makes a contract very unstable. It allows a sponsor or angler to terminate the relationship within 30 days after a written notice. Few of my contracts have out clauses. I've never quit a sponsor, so I've never needed an out clause. But I have been discontinued from a few contracts for certain reasons —bad economic times, poor tournament performance.

I experienced my toughest year with sponsor support in 1989. I hadn't made the BASS Masters Classic in two years (missing it by less than a pound both years). At that point, I had eight sponsors that I had worked hard to promote for a lot of years.

It was also in 1989 that the economy started to spiral downward and the fishing industry went sour. Four of the eight sponsors sent me "Dear John" letters exercising the out clause or simply decided not to renew my contract.

That was a real difficult time. At that time, I had just bought a new house and I had a pretty healthy house payment. And I was trying to furnish this brand new house, so I had a lot of major expenditures. And Diane and I were planning marriage at that time.

Those letters came in all in a three-month period right before Christmas. I remember how devastating it was. All I could think about was—"the bottom line is you don't lose your house." I was concerned about winning enough money to make my payments.

At first I was real mad. Then I had a little bit of self pity. I worried and I was down at the mouth for a few days. Then I thought, well, there's got to be a better way to handle this situation. Instead of sending a nasty letter or making a nasty phone call, I tried to get my job back with every company.

Each company was cordial and friendly. But there was no longer any room in their promotional budget for Joe Thomas. So I sent each one of them a letter stating that I understood it was poor economic times. I understood that my performance had been sub-par and those two things in combination led up to my termination. But I wanted them to know that the bottom line was that I was in this business for the long haul and — whether they were with me or not — I was going to stay. I told them that I appreciated their years of support to me and I would be back. They would see my name again.

The rest was history. I went on to make the Classic that year and won the Red Man All American. I got two of those four former sponsors back — and signed eight new sponsors. I have fourteen sponsors that I work with at the current time.

When it comes to attracting endorsement contracts, I feel that image is extremely important. I've worked hard to project a good, clean, all-American image.

Don't get the impression that once you win a big tournament that sponsors come knocking your door down. Attracting sponsors and then keeping them happy is a full-time job. I go hunting a few weeks a year, but other than that I work 300 days a year. I spend hours at my desk trying to keep up with the sponsors' commitments and keep everybody happy. I aggressively seek speaking engagements.

And every two months, I send a report to my sponsors that lets them know what I have been doing to promote myself and their products. I send them photocopies of everything that I have been involved in — print, photographs or advertisements in the last two months. Some photos show their logo. Some stories mention their name in print. I also send tape recordings of radio shows where I have mentioned their name. Some of these things don't even mention their company, but I still want them to know that I am out there representing their company.

I'm proud of the way I promote my sponsors' products and keep their interests in the forefront of what I do. I'll never say I'm as good a fisherman as there is out there, but I'll put my promotional skills up there against any bass pro.

Much of that promotion comes with speaking at seminars, boat shows and tackle store appearances. I've tried to integrate a good speaking seminar with a very soft sell approach — almost a subliminal selling approach. There's nothing that the public hates more than a hard sell. The only company logos I wear are very subtle golf-type logos on a sweater, on a collar, on a sleeve. I don't wear what we call tournament "scare shirts," to do a seminar because, in my opinion, that's overkill and makes the audience skeptical.

I do try to mention Stren line and Zebco reels and All Star Rods when appropriate, and every lure I throw. It's all in a lightly presented message to the people. But I teach them how to catch fish. Then, they come up and ask about those products.

In preparation for this particular part of professional fishing, I took several public speaking courses in college. It seemed like I had a little bit of talent at speaking. I didn't have to work as hard at speech class and creative writing classes as I did at courses like math and chemistry. If you're a young guy and a career in professional fishing is your goal, I would advise getting at least two years of college under your belt. Take creative writing and public speaking courses.

College will help you a lot and give you something to fall back on. I would suggest a business, marketing or communications degree. If you're already out of school and want to improve your communications skills, there are a lot of night courses at colleges that you can take.

I've been told many times by some of my bigger sponsors that it is possible to have too many sponsors. To some people, 14 sponsors are too many. And some of my fellow anglers say that is too many to handle properly.

I don't believe that. It's like saying you can't fish three tournament circuits. I've been doing it for nine years. You can do it. You just have to work a lot harder. You just don't get to take as many days off.

The bottom line is Joe Thomas is not a Larry Nixon or a Gary Klein. I don't have a TV show like Charlie Ingram or Hank Parker. These guys are receiving large chunks of money from four or five accounts like Team Brunswick, Tracker/Nitro Boats and Wrangler. I don't have those big companies.

So I have to make up for it by doing a good job for a lot of companies,

Seminars and show appearances have become a big part of our sport.

both big and small. I supplement my income by working with a lot of lure companies (non-conflicting lure companies) and products that are unique. An example of a unique product with a special, distinctive niche is one called Hook Away. It's a little lure cover that you put on the treble hooks of a lure. It keeps your rods from tangling — you know what a nightmare rod lockers can be. The public is bananas over it because it keeps your lures safe and away from the kids.

Other examples are the Speedo Bead and Simpleton Sinker from U.S. Tackle. These are quick-on, quick-off sinker and Carolina stop system. They're very unique little items.

Endorsement monies from these smaller, unique companies all add up. And maybe the product will go big and I will grow with it. That would be cool.

I've had some good accounts and still do — like Skeeter, Yamaha, DuPont, Rubbermaid, Zebco, and Dodge trucks. Dodge was one of my accounts that brought a tear to my eye when they let the whole Skeeter team go. That was the hardest sponsor to lose, because it was a very good deal. Use of a vehicle each year is especially appreciated in this business.

It is encouraging to see major companies like Rubbermaid getting involved with our sport. Rubbermaid has been the official cooler of the Classic for several years now and began sponsoring the Rubbermaid Bassmaster Casting Kids national contest in 1992. Even more exciting for me personally is that Rubbermaid jumped into the tackle box market in early 1993 with their ProSeries and I am fortunate enough to be a member of their pro staff. It's easy to promote and recommend high quality products like Rubbermaid.

It takes both big and small companies to make the fishing business go. So I don't treat Hook Away any different than I do Zebco.

Lets talk about money. You won't hear or read much about the financial side of professional bass fishing — like you do with other sports stars. I'll bet you've often wondered just how much a Rick Clunn makes or even a Joe Thomas makes in a year. Well, I'm going to give you some ballpark figures to show you just how far this sport has come.

I would estimate that the tournament earnings per year for an above-average fisherman like Mike Folkestad, Greg Hines or myself is probably about $35,000 a year. That's not a lot of money when you consider that it can cost $25,000 to $30,000 a year in expenses to fish the B.A.S.S. and other tournament trails.

I made less than $30,000 in tournament earnings in 1991 - a big drop from $180,000 in 1990. Thanks goodness for sponsors.

Endorsement contracts provide the foundation for almost any successful fishing career. But with a few exceptions, these sponsorships aren't nearly as lucrative as some fishing fans believe. Here are some examples.

The top fishermen probably make somewhere around $300 to $500 monthly from lure, line and rod-and-reel manufacturers (on the average).

The big money comes from a major contract with a boat or a motor company. You're talking about anywhere from a $10,000 to $100,000 a year contract for the very top individuals in this sport. You're talking about a handful of individuals that are getting that kind of money — and you can probably guess who they are.

Most of the more lucrative deals involve boat and motor companies, but aren't limited to those. For example, a member of Team Brunswick has a package deal that involves a boat, outboard, trolling motor, rods and reels.

Most of the top pros have taken advantage of package

An on-the-water photo session with a writer.

programs, a relatively new trend in the fishing business in recent years. Companies like Brunswick and OMC spent all sorts of money buying up boat companies like you and I collect lures. That enables a guy like Gary Klein or Shaw Grigsby to enjoy financially rewarding packages that includes boats, outboard, trolling motors and rods and reels.

There aren't many of those deals out there. But it gives you something to dream about.

In contrast, an angler who is just starting out is doing well if he can get a company to discount products, or provide a few free items. Keep in mind that this stuff doesn't grow on trees and these companies are trying to make a profit.

Here's the bottom line on the sport of professional fishing when it comes to endorsements: there are about 40 guys who are making over $25,000 a year in endorsements. Less than 30 of them are knocking out better than $50,000 a year. I would estimate that about 20 guys top the $75,000 mark. And there are probably five to 10 pros who are knocking out more than six figures in endorsements. I fall somewhere in the middle in there.

Speaking engagements, for me, are very important
First there's the immediate monetary gain — it pays very well. A seminar speaker can expect to be paid anywhere from $400—$1,000 a day. If you've just won the BASS Masters Classic, you might be able to get a couple of thousand a day. That would be short-lived, though, unless you get to be a Roland Martin or Hank Parker.

When it comes to speaking engagements, my target number

is 30 days. Last year I think I did 43 days. I aim for X number of speaking dollars in my budget.

Then there are free promotional days for your sponsors, which is written into each standard contract. I had a couple of weeks in the fall where I did nothing but attend sponsor functions. It cut into my hunting time and nobody loves to hunt more than Joe Thomas. But that's all a part of my business.

Sponsors require a certain amount of free days for functions like the Skeeter Jamboree, Yamaha Elite Angler tournament and pro team meetings with DuPont and Zebco. I did 12 or 13 days of these this past fall in a very short period of time.

I am my own agent. We haven't seen much penetration by sports agents in professional bass fishing. And the few that are around haven't made significant strides in attracting non-fishing related companies (like Coke or Nike).

Really, there is only one good fishing agent out there and his stable includes Larry Nixon, Denny Brauer, Tommy Martin, Shaw Grigsby and some of the other top dogs. In a situation like that, I am afraid that I would be on the back burner.

I pursued a sports marketing agency in Cincinnati to solicit outside the industry account. My agreement was that they would not touch the fishing industry companies. Their role was to solicit accounts from outside of the fishing industry. It's been a year and a half, they haven't gotten me the first deal. I think I'm lost in the shuffle again. They've got Anthony Munoz of the Bengals, Chris Sabo of the Reds, Darryl Strawberry of the Dodgers and a couple of pro golfers. I think fishermen and their income fall so far down the list that any possible commissions from my career are so low that they aren't real interested. They come up with an idea every now and then, but it just never materializes. I think they just want me to know that I'm still on their books.

I'm convinced, however that some agent is going to come into this sport and bring in big bucks from Coca-Cola or Nike with them. All it takes is for somebody to get in the right door and push the right button with the right person.

So I serve as my own agent, which gives me the freedom to pick and choose my speaking dates.

Last year, I did 43 appearances in 28 cities. That's a lot when you consider that I fished four tournaments in that three-month period also.

The show season is a short one — January, February, March and the first two weeks of April. That's when most sports shows are held. I never have a weekend open in that three-month period and I often don't have an open weekday. I rarely have a blank spot in my calendar during that three-month period, although it gets awfully hectic at times (check out my February schedule on pages 136 and 137 to see what I mean).

That sounds dumb, I know. But consider that a pro can make anywhere from $400 to $1,000 a day (and I fall somewhere in the middle, again) for doing speaking engagements. Turn on your calculator for a second. You figure that 30 or 40 speaking engagements can produce about $20,000 to $25,000 in a three-month period of time. That's as much as a lot of people make in a year.

For the young pro who is just starting out, the easiest way to work your way to such speaking engage-

I never get tired of getting requests for my autograph.

ments is to build a reputation locally. Think locally and regionally before worrying about a national reputation. That's what I did. I was known as a good bass fisherman and a good seminar speaker in Cincinnati before I was in demand for national appearances.

You have to be a hero locally before you can be a hero nationally. There are a few exceptions like Kevin VanDam. What people don't realize about Kevin VanDam is that he was a hero in Kalamazoo, Mich., and that he won every tournament in Michigan for two or three years. He was a local hero first — but it didn't take long

February

Monday	Tuesday	Wednesday
3 Travel Day	**4** Seminar — Kansas City	**5** Travel Day
10 Travel Day	**11** Columbus Sports Show	**12** National Marine Manuf. Assn. Show — St. Louis
17 Tournament Practice	**18** Tournament Practice	**19** Tournament Competition
24 Indy Sports Show	**25** Indy Sports Show	**26** Indy Sports Show

1992

Thursday	Friday	Saturday	Sunday
	Travel Day	**1** Seminar — Charleston, S.C.	**2** Seminar — Roanoke, Va.
6 Prefish — Golden Blend Tuscaloosa, Ala.	**7** Golden Blend Prefish	**8** Golden Blend Prefish	**9** Golden Blend Prefish
13 NMMA Show — St. Louis	**14** NMMA Show — St. Louis	**15** Travel Day	**16** B.A.S.S. Pro Am— Jacksonville
20 Tournament Competition	**21** Tournament Competition	**22** Tournament Competition	**23** Travel Day
27 Travel Day	**28** Travel Day	**29** Seminar — Wooster, Mass.	

for him to dominate on a bigger stage.

I attacked all of the tournament circuits (the viable ones) in my area. I fished them heavily and stayed after them pretty hard. I also did some things like getting to know the local outdoors press.

My co-author Tim Tucker, who has covered the national tournament circuit for more than a decade as a senior writer for BASSMASTER Magazine, tells me that I was the first pro to put together a press kit for both the press and (both current and prospective) sponsors.

The press kit was a great idea by my ex-girlfriend, Becky Wing. Wing Media was her dad's company and she and I decided that there had to be an avenue, a way to package and sell yourself and stand out from the crowd. The press kit was a big part of my promotional package.

I learned a lot about promotion from Becky and pro Rich Tauber, who is a very good business-minded fisherman from California and one of my best friends (and a guy who has probably done more for me than anybody in this business). Rich may be the best promoter in the industry.

We used Wing Media as an avenue. She marketed and packaged me and helped with some of my contracts. She also picked out stationery and business cards. All those things that I didn't think you needed. She even wrote press releases. I didn't know the first thing about a press release.

I was 24 at the time and my career was just starting. But we got my press materials into the newspapers and local magazines like Ohio Fisherman and Tri-State Fisherman.

A lot of fishermen look at dealing with the press as a necessary evil. I enjoy it. Publicity and exposure are the lifeblood of my profession.

There is no better way to make Joe Thomas a household name in fishing than to have him included in every piece of print that you pick up. I die for articles in BASSMASTER. You've got to really be a winner to get a lot of things in BASSMASTER, but I've been in it and a lot of other publications.

Bass Fishing Magazine, which used to be called Cast, is the Operation Bass/Red Man magazine. For several years after I had won the Red Man All American, you couldn't pick up a copy of it without seeing either a picture or a quote from me.

You'll find the Larry Nixons and Rick Clunns and Guido Hibdons in BASSMASTER. I think it's just an extra level that you've

A good relationship with the press is the foundation of any fishing career.

got to move to. But I'll take all of the publicity I can get.

It all starts with the local newspaper outdoor writers. We've got three or four of them around the tri-state area where I live, along with local and regional outdoors magazines.

Some of the best advice I can give is to get to know these local writers. Don't be afraid to take them out in the boat with you, even if it is a little inconvenient. If a writer calls you for a story, be receptive. Make them feel like they are important and that you want to spend time with them. If you've got to drive and meet them, drive and meet them. Sit down with them. Don't be afraid to do a phone interview.

The best guide I've seen for aspiring pros, club anglers, guides and even tournament directors who want to make more money at fishing is entitled "The Bass Pro Workshop: How to Promote Yourself and Attract Sponsors." It is three hours of audio cassettes and a workbook with sample letters and such that will smooth the bumps out of your ride to getting more bucks from fishing. I don't have any affiliation with this program — but I recommend it highly (for more information, write The Bass Catalog, Rt. 2, Box 177, Micanopy, Fla. 32667; telephone 1-800-252-FISH).

As you can see, there's a lot more to the business of professional fishing than just catching fish. The most successful bass pros are also the best business men.

Chapter 13

Casting About
For $150,000

Golden Blend World Championship
April 3-4, 1992
Lake Tuscaloosa

MARCH 30th

The University of Alabama and the city of Tuscaloosa will be our home for the next week as I prepare to compete for the biggest prize in tournament fishing — $150,000 in cash and a Chevy truck. It's the Golden Blend Diamond Invitational World Bass Championship, the crowning event on the other national tournament trail.

I'm glad to be here. The Golden Blend championship will be one of the highlights of my year. I worked hard to get here, finishing in the top 10 in four of the five Golden Blend events I fished to qualify fourth in the eastern division. It's always great to qualify for any championship tournament, but the money — that pot at the end of this rainbow — makes it even more exciting.

There is plenty of competition among the 40 qualifiers for this tournament. Most of the big names are here — the Rick Clunns, Guido Hibdons, Denny Brauers and Shaw Grigsbys. So I'll have my work cut out for me. But I'm anxious to get started.

Diane and I arrived early this morning and visited with my friend Mike Redding who I had fished with before the off-limits period. Mike lives on Lake Tuscaloosa and knows quite a bit about it. Today, I was just trying to get some water level information. We talked a lot about baits that had been working pretty well. Just general patterns and theories. Not so much about individual spots because I wanted to avoid such talk.

We checked in and found that we have a really nice room. It's a nice facility for a tournament. The boats are all identical Rangers with Evinrudes — just like in the BASS Masters Classic. They are located right across the courtyard. We're on the campus of the University of Alabama in a three-story hotel, which is really nice because we don't have a high-rise to deal with or anything like that. We can get our tackle from the boat to the hotel pretty easily and we have a secure parking lot where we can park our vehicles without the bother of a parking garage.

It's just a really good set-up. Most of our meals and events are going to be right here in the hotel so we don't have to do a lot of running around according to the itinerary looked.

My mom, dad and brother are going to come down in a couple of days to watch the weigh-ins, so I get to be with them a little bit, which will be nice. It's going to be kind of hectic with all of the practice and the press and that kind of thing. I won't get to see them a whole lot.

We had a boat-orientation meeting tonight. It is freezing cold outside. The wind is just howling. It had been very warm, but this little cold front is coming through and the forecast is for rain during the next several days.

It looks like it is going to rain all the way up through the tournament, which would suit me. The more overcast it is and the more it rains, the better those fish will come up on a stickbait or a spinnerbait, which is what I am counting on for this tournament. I'm praying it won't be a sight-fishing tournament. I can't afford that. The cloudier and nastier it is, the better I will like it.

Got in bed about 9:30.

MARCH 31st

The first day of practice. My press observer was Jeff Frischkorn from Cleveland, Ohio. I have practiced with Jeff previously in the BASS Masters Classic and other events. He's a good guy to be with. Very positive attitude and asks a lot of good questions.

It was cloudy, windy, rainy and overcast today. I caught quite a few fish, which I expected on a day like today. Down in the clear water in the lower end of the lake is where I fished, 90 percent of my strikes came on a gold Smithwick Rattlin' Rogue with a black back and orange belly. I was fishing it on 10-pound Stren line and just snapping it within about 2 to 3 feet under the surface after making a long cast. I had several 3-pounders and a lot of 2-pounders today. And I had a lot of fish come up and flash on the lure — nice fish that just didn't take the bait.

Several times, I hooked one fish and had a couple of fish following him. So there is a lot of fish in the areas that I'm fishing. I've noticed that the mouths of the coves, the steep bluff-type of banks at the mouths of the coves, seemed to be the trick.

The largemouths are a little harder to come by, but it will take the heavier weight from a few largemouths to win this tournament. The spotted bass only average about 13 inches long, which is not going to do much good in this tournament. We're going to have some of those 3-pound largemouths.

I really believe that if the weather keeps warming up and it stays cloudy and breezy like they are predicting that the bigger bass will bite.

I haven't stayed in any one area very long. I've covered a lot of water today. Just made lots of casts. I tried to find several areas that are productive.

I feel pretty good after the first day of practice. My nerves are very calm. I'm not really too concerned. I thought the $150,000 top prize would start to bug me, but it hasn't so far.

We had dinner tonight in the room. Diane wasn't feeling very well. This pregnancy has got her stomach churned up. She's got a cold, which she picked up on the road somewhere. I bailed out on dinner and just stayed in the room and ordered room service. Just going to get some good rest.

I'm boat No. 3 out in the second flight tomorrow, so I can sleep a little bit later. We're supposed to be at the boats at 6 a.m. tomorrow. Today we were there at 5:30 a.m. It's about 9:15 now. We're going to turn in and get a real good night's sleep.

APRIL 1st

Second day of practice. Pretty disappointing day. I really expected to be able to go up in the dirtier water and catch them well today. The water temperature was in the mid- to upper-60s, depending on what part of the lake you were in.

The water is dirty in the upper river. A lot of grass, but the fish just don't seem to want to bite. I covered a lot of water up there, mainly flipping and throwing a spinnerbait.

143

It was kind of funny, because my press observer today had fished with Jay Yelas yesterday. At the end of the day, he made the comment that I had fished almost every pocket that Yelas had fished the day before. They hadn't caught anything either. We struggled to catch a very few keepers. Nothing of any size. I was really surprised with all of the good-looking places where I flipped that jig and lizard in that shallow cover that I couldn't get a big fish to bite.

A lot of to anglers fishing were up there in the dirty water, trying to put together a big largemouth pattern. I think everybody realizes that the jerkbait fish in the clear water are probably not going to be worth much if there is a largemouth bite up in the river.

The weather forecasters are starting to change their tune on the weather. They're saying it might be sunny for the tournament. If it is and we don't have a whole lot of wind, I'm afraid those sight fishermen are going to really hammer the rest of us.

Sight-fishing is not my thing. It never has been. It is one of my weaknesses. I just don't chose to fish that way. I have trouble seeing the fish on the beds. I'm more of a mover and cover-type of fisherman. I'm just afraid these weather conditions are playing right into the sight-fishermen's hands. Everybody talks about seeing a lot of fish on the nest. Guido Hibdon, Dion Hibdon, Shaw Grigsby and Paul Elias really think that the tournament is going to be won by bed fishing. It puts me in a very concerned state. I'm a lot more nervous tonight that I was yesterday.

We're getting ready to go to dinner tonight. Then we have a concert with Robin Lee, a country singer. My parents are going to go with us. We are going to try to have a relaxing evening.

Tomorrow is press day — a day off of the tournament water. We are supposed to be up at 7 a.m. and go over to a marina on the Warrior River. We'll work with the press doing interviews and posing for pictures and the rest of the day will be free. I'll spend the rest of the day just getting tackle ready and relaxing a little bit.

Diane is still not feeling well. I'm kind of worried about her a little bit, with her being with child and all.

APRIL 2nd

Press day. It's been a long day. We spent the morning at the marina on the Warrior River working with the press. I got a lot of story material done today with several different writers.

Afterwards, I came back and worked on my tackle for a while. My brother played golf with Paul Elias, Ron Shuffield and Johnny Borden and a few of the guys. He had a good time. I went to

A cold front hit Tuscaloosa, but these small spotted bass kept hitting a jerkbait.

lunch with my mom and dad and Diane. We got to sit and talk for a while. That was kind of nice.

I'm beginning to feel myself tightening up. I just don't know if this jerkbait pattern is going to pan out. It was sunny today and there were guys walking around the docks at the marina during the press function snatching 3- and 4-pound largemouths off the beds. If they are biting that good on the beds there, I know they are going to be biting that good in Lake Tuscaloosa. The weather forecast predicts sunny skies and light winds tomorrow, which is absolutely the worst thing that could happen to me and my jerkbait pattern.

Some wind and even a little cloud cover would make a big difference. It's very irritating. It seems like every time I need the weather to do something, it does just the opposite. It's just been one of those years. But maybe I can still make it happen and get the right bite. All it takes is one 5- or 6-pounder and you are in the ballgame if you can put together a limit to go with it.

I spent about three hours spooling my rods and reels and doing my tackle. Checking everything over. I'm going to be prepared no matter what happens.

Tomorrow is the start of the tournament. I'm in the third boat out, so I'm right up front. I'm fishing with a guy named Tim Tucker tomorrow. You ever heard of that guy? Just kidding. Tim Tucker is a senior writer for BASSMASTER Magazine and the co-author of this book we're compiling. Being from Florida, he's upset because it's going to be cold tomorrow and he didn't bring his snowsuit. Well, I didn't pack for him, doggone it. Anyway, I've got to quit ragging on those outdoor writers. They're okay guys.

Tomorrow is the opening gun. The start of the biggest tournament ever as far as payout is concerned.

APRIL 3rd

First day of competition. It doesn't look like I'm going to be winning this one. I didn't have a banner day today. It was cold and bright and sunny and calm — all the things I had prayed wouldn't happen. I caught four bass that weighed 4 pounds, 11 ounces.

It was a very disappointing day at best. I stayed with my game plan to throw that jerkbait and cover a lot of water. I did get a lot of looks at that Rogue. A lot of interested bass, but few takers.

My press observer Tim Tucker said that I caught 13 fish today, but only four were keepers. I caught my best fish late in the afternoon off a little clump of grass on a steep bank that I had fished several times and caught some nice ones in practice.

It was amazing the number of 2— and 3-pound fish that would come up and flash and roll on my bait, but did not get the lure in their mouth. I guess that's what kept me throwing that Rogue all day long — the fact that I was getting some response to that lure.

I just knew that anytime the water would warm up a degree or two more or the wind would blow a little harder and I would get a 4-pounder to come up and take it. It's that time of the year...

Tournament Tip

Fishing for spawning bass in the spring can be a very effective pattern and it is frequently a tournament winner. The majority of the bass found in a lake or river system usually spawn on the first full moon phase after the water reaches 65 degrees. Normally, shallow, clear water pockets are prime spawning areas. Bass choose sheltered areas out of the wind the majority of the time. Vegetation or overhanging limbs are normally chosen to bed under. A grub, tubejig or jerkbait are the most productive lures during the spring of the year.

It's just so disappointing to have them flashing on the bait and not eating it. But I stayed with it most of the day. I did break for one hour and ran to the river and flipped.

Then it calmed down and got very flat and sunny in the afternoon and my strikes diminished. I caught one small fish flipping a lizard up in the river. I just couldn't stay with it. I didn't feel comfortable, I wasn't getting any big bites up there, so I came back down and threw the Rogue for the last two hours. I managed to catch one fish in the 2-pound range. I ended up with one largemouth and three spotted bass.

Randy Dearman is leading the tournament with 16 pounds. He is obviously sight-fishing from the way he was talking — as were most of the leaders today. I'm 11 pounds down entering tomorrow's final round of competition. That's a lot of weight to even think of making up, especially on this lake.

Paul Elias is second with 14 pounds and Zell Rowland is third with 12. Shaw Grigsby, Guido Hibdon and Dion Hibdon are in the top 10. All of them are throwing finesse baits to bass they can see.

The wind is supposed to blow a little harder tomorrow. I'm just hoping that I can coax a few of those fish that have been flashing on my bait to take it. I'm just going to fish hard. I'm going to stay doing the same thing. Otherwise, I don't know anything to do to change other than sight-fishing, but I haven't located any bedding fish. So I'm just going to go out and catch the best stringer I can.

Operation Bass is paying 10 places in this tournament. I'm going to try for one of those paychecks. Who knows what will happen. If it gets really tough on the sight-fishermen — which could happen because a lot of bedding bass have been caught. If I get a couple of the right bites, anything can happen.

I'm very disappointed. It's just been a tough day. But I'm trying not to let it bother me and keep my attitude right and make as good a showing as I can.

Operation Bass officials are not going to let everybody weigh in tomorrow in front of the crowd. If you are not in the top 10, you're not going to weigh in. Quite honestly, that bothers me a little bit. I worked awfully darn hard to get here and deserve the right to represent my sponsors during the weigh-in, regardless of whether I'm fifth or 25th in the standings.

I'm not trying to beat on Operation Bass. It has been a real good organization for a long time. They've been very good to me. I'm not one to question the way things are done much. I usually just do my job and keep my mouth shut. That's what I'll continue to do.

Let's get out of politics and talk about fishing. I'm going to go out and catch the best stringer on the Rogue I can. Maybe I'll get a 12- or 14-pound bag and make myself happy.

I'm hoping to get in from the weigh-in in time to catch part of the University of Cincinnati's game with Michigan. They're in the Final Four of the NCAA basketball tournament, which is big stuff back home.

I'm just trying to act like I'm not really tense. I'm tense.

Diane is feeling a little bit better, by the way. We're going to hit the hay by about 10.

APRIL 4th

The final day of competition. Zell Rowland won it with two very consistent stringers. He had about 12 pounds each day. As I listened in the press conference, it was obvious that eight out of the top 10 finishers were sight-fishing. Just about everybody caught them on a G-4, one of Guido Hibdon's tubebaits with Shaw Grigsby's High Performance Hook — sight-fishing spawning largemouths.

I had a little better day today. I had five bass that weighed about 7 pounds. I caught 10 keepers doing the same thing as yesterday. Again, I had a lot of good fish turning on my bait, flashing on it.

My press partner said that I made more casts than he's ever seen anybody make. Of course, the Rogue is a very fast bait. He said I averaged 180 casts an hour and I made 43

Winning Ways

Better known as a power-bait fisherman, Zell Rowland switched gears and turned to a finesse lure for sight fishing to catch 23 pounds, 3 ounces, and win the biggest prize in fishing. Rowland utilized a chartreuse-colored G4 tubejig with a light bullet weight on a 1/0 High Performance hook on 8-pound test line. He saw every bass he caught in 1 to 3 feet of water. The top six anglers in this tournament scored by sight-fishing for spawners and pre-spawn bass.

boat moves during the day. I don't know if that is an impressive or unimpressive statistic. It didn't produce as well as it probably should have, but it was better than yesterday. I finished 15th in the tournament — just a pound or two away from a top-10 finish and a check.

Dion Hibdon's catch today was disqualified because he allowed his press partner Sammy Lee to help him land a fish, which is against the rules in this type of tournament. He apparently didn't know the rules. It wasn't a blatant deception type of thing, but the video crew recorded it on film and it really cost him. With his catch, Dion would have finished in third place. But his disqualification enabled Randy Dearman to finish third behind Paul Elias and Dion fell completely out of the top 10.

I stayed on the lower end of the lake. I literally started right at the takeoff site, just outside the off-limits area in the real clear water. I lost the first fish that I hooked, a 2-pound largemouth. I fought him quite a while and he just pulled off at the boat. I ended up catching about 25 fish, including 10 keepers. I just couldn't get those big ones to eat that Rogue.

I have to believe that the water is just a few degrees away from that happening. Usually a Rogue is best in water temperature in the mid-60s and right around pre-spawn. Maybe these fish are too far into the spawn. Maybe they've passed the point of eating it. We've had a couple of cold fronts come through and I think that slowed their metabolism down a little bit.

They'll flash at it and look at it and swirl at it and do all kinds of strange things, but they won't eat it. That's what kept me hooked a jerkbait for the two days of the tournament. That was my probably my downfall, but I really felt it was my best chance of doing well in the tournament and I stayed with it.

Who knows what would have happened under a little different conditions. If the clouds and the wind had shown up, those guys wouldn't have been able to see those fish on the bed and my fish might have been more aggressive. It might have been a whole different ballgame, but that's the way things are.

To add insult to injury, the University of Cincinnati lost to Michigan in the final couple of minutes. It wasn't a very good day for me.

We're planning to pack up and head out early in the morning. I've got a tax appointment on Monday to do my taxes. Then I've got a couple of seminars coming up, so I can't fool around. I really need to get home.

And then it will be time to get back on the B.A.S.S. circuit and renew my efforts to return to the Classic. That's the goal of every touring pro.

Chapter 14

A Healthy Dose
Of Disappointment

Alabama Bassmaster Invitational
April 15-17, 1992
Lake Guntersville

APRIL 11th

After doing an all-day seminar at Wiley's Sporting Goods in Huntsville, we checked in at the Best Western in Guntersville. I've been spending the last two and a half hours or so working on my tackle. The boat is all ready and cleaned up.

Diane spent most of that time unpacking our clothes, getting them into the drawers and just getting settled. We didn't feel much like going anywhere. Dinner was at a Pizza Hut next door.

My plan tomorrow is to drive all the way up to Mud Creek. They're predicting some fog in the morning. I know I won't be able to run the lake very well, so I'm going to drive up there and put in. I think to hit a home run in this tournament I'm probably going to need to fish the upper end of the lake. The water temperature is near 70. With a full moon coming on, the fish will probably be in a pre-spawn mode.

There is very little grass in the lake from what I'm told. I'm going to concentrate my efforts on stumps and laydowns and other wooden structure in the pockets off the main river and just see what happens.

APRIL 12th

First day of practice. It was 5:30 a.m. as I headed north to a boat ramp in Mud Creek. It's Sunday and there were a lot of locals launching there. It was so foggy you couldn't see anything. I've never fished Mud Creek before, so I fished around blindly in the fog with probably 30 other boats.

There were a lot of other tournament boats there. Most of us were there for the potential of the grass in those creeks since there's not much grass on the lower end of the lake. Early in the fog, I managed to catch a couple of pretty nice fish by slow-rolling a spinnerbait in some patches of grass that were 50 to 100 yards offshore.

I watched a local angler catch a 7-pound bass and another guy lose one almost as big, so obviously there's some big-fish potential here in that Mud Creek area. I left there and ended up running main river pockets most of the day as I worked my way up the lake.

Once the fog cleared at about 10 a.m., it was sunny and fairly breezy. I alternated between a spinnerbait, a jerkbait and a plastic lizard as I bounced from pocket to pocket. I was really amazed that I didn't do better than I did. I caught fish fairly sporadically, except for one small creek where a 3- and 5-pounder came out of one area on a black-and-blue jig. I think it's got the potential to produce a big stringer, but you'd really have to gamble to run up and fish it. I'm going to have to see what the lower end has to hold, but this is a real good area. It's got a boat ramp in it, so it could get a lot fishing pressure from local anglers.

It was dark when I trailered back to the Best Western, showered and drove to the tournament registration. After we got registered, we grabbed some Arby's on the way in. It's about 10 p.m. now. I'm just really tired. I did a lot of driving, a lot of traveling today. It's starting to get later in the spring, so the days are a lot longer.

APRIL 13th

Second day of practice. I launched the boat about 6 a.m. and unhooked my boat trailer so Diane could use the van today. She and a friend wanted to go shopping in town. I don't blame her. She's probably bored stiff sitting in the hotel room. She can't go out in the boat with me now because she's more than six months pregnant. I'm just afraid for her to go out even today when I'm staying close by. I'm afraid of hitting a wave and jarring her and hurting the baby. I'm probably too paranoid. That's just the way I feel about it.

152

I fished the lower one-third of Lake Guntersville, today, concentrating on Honeycomb and Brown creeks in particular.

It was sunny, windy and 75 degrees, just a beautiful day. I was amazed at the lack of boat traffic on the lower end. I saw few tournament boats. I managed to catch several nice fish by snapping a Rogue around shallow stumps near deep water.

That pattern produced nine keepers in the 2- to 3 1/2-pound range. I was pretty surprised at the quality of the fish. But I shouldn't be surprised at what the Rogue can do. It gets a lot of bites. It's been real good to me.

I feel pretty comfortable that I could stay down on this lower end and catch a nice stringer if the wind would blow and things stay right. I was pleased that I didn't see much fishing pressure in the area.

Diane met me at the ramp at about 6:30 p.m. A Pizza Hut spaghetti dinner and we're in for the night. Diane showed me some of the things that she bought today shopping. I'm only going to make her take half of them back... just kidding.

APRIL 14th

Final practice day. I trailered about halfway up the lake to Mink Creek. I wanted a full day so I got up extra early and I was on the water before daylight. I really worked hard today from the Mink Creek area, which is mid-lake, up to about Mud Creek.

I checked a place where I've caught them consistently over the years. It's a little grass drop where the main river channel makes a slight bend in front of South Sauty Creek. It's on a river ledge where the water drops from 4 to 25 feet. This spot has some really good green millfoil growing on the edge.

I saw very few boats fishing that area as I fished it early in the morning. I caught three fish in the 3-pound class on a Rat-L-Trap in 10 minutes before leaving the area. I moved down about a quarter-mile on the same ledge and I caught one about 2 pounds in 15 casts. I have to believe that it is a really prime spot. I've caught a lot of big fish there over the years in tournaments. I think this is the kind of place you could go in every morning and probably catch a nice limit of fish — maybe 10 to 14 pounds, if the wind doesn't blow too hard.

From there, I basically ran the backs of creeks looking for grass patches. I found one little area of grass near Mud Creek that had a lot of fish on it. It's amazing how they group up in the grass. My only big bite of the day came fishing an isolated duck blind in a bay off the Mud Creek. I fished the grass all around it without getting a strike. But when I slow-rolled a 1/2-ounce spinnerbait through the middle of the blind, a 7-pounder pounced on it.

I caught a pretty good limit on both ends of the lake. But I feel more comfortable with the mid-lake section and that grassy river ledge.

At the partners pairing meeting, I came into some good fortune. You work really hard and then every now and then something falls in your lap. It was there that I found out that Rubbermaid, which is the B.A.S.S. cooler sponsors, plans to get into the tackle box market and is putting together a pro team and they want me to be a part of it. That's the kind of company that anybody would want to be associated with.

My partner is a Florida pro who has been catching some fish in the same section of the lake I want to fish. He feels we can catch a good stringer on that main river channel. I feel good about that.

A quick meal is followed by an hour working on my tackle. I've got the alarm set for 5 a.m.

APRIL 15th

First day of competition. Today was one of those partly cloudy, breezy, hazy, gorgeous fishing days that you just pray for when you're on a bunch of fish. I managed to catch a good number of fish today, but wasn't able to get my kicker.

I started the day on my main river ledge out in front of North Sauty Creek. I pulled up on the river drop at about 7 a.m. and I was the only boat on the end of it. I was really shocked that there weren't more boats out there, since I was in the last flight. At 8:20 I was culling. I ended up catching about 14 or 15 keepers on that spot with a 1/2-ounce chrome-and-blue Rat-L-Trap. When I got my first strike of the day, I immediately dropped a marker and fished around it.

From there, I had some kind of action on almost every other cast. Nothing was over 2 pounds, but an early limit felt good. And I didn't lose a single fish, which can be credited to switching to a fiberglass All Star GT2 rod. Glass rods are better suited for fast-moving lures like a Rat-L-Trap because they are less sensitive and react slower to violent movements of the fish.

I waited around until my partner could catch five bass before we moved north to my big-fish creek. We were greeted by a tremendous thunderstorm, which made fishing difficult. I managed to cull two fish there, though.

We returned to the river ledge, but the wind was up and the fishing weren't biting. And another boat was sitting right on my best area. Rather than cut him off, which I didn't think would be right, I fell in behind him and I watched his partner lose a giant bass — 6 or 8 pounds — on a spinnerbait.

Lake Guntersville remains a great fishery despite the disappearance of the milfoil.

The tournament pro in the front of the boat hollered to me that this was his best area. I asked him why — if this was his best spot — he wasn't here the first few hours this morning. He didn't respond. After a tense couple of seconds, I think he got the message. I don't think I'll have any problem with him tomorrow.

My seven fish today weighed 12 pounds — and that's not even in the top 50. It's amazing how many fish were caught today. Thirty pounds is leading the tournament, if you can believe that. Six fish that weighed 30 pounds. Second place is 25 pounds. Just to be in the money you had to have almost 13 pounds.

I drew Lonnie Stanley for tomorrow. I'm kind of in a weird situation. He is way up there in the Classic standings and had 13 pounds, so I'm going to ride with him. He said we could fish my area first thing in the morning, then he had some good Carolina-rig spots where we can finish our limit or upgrade a small limit. So that's the plan for tomorrow morning.

I'm really tired. Diane told me I'm not been paying enough attention to her lately. Maybe I haven't been paying enough attention to her. It's 9:30 p.m. Five-thirty will be here before you know it.

APRIL 16th

Second competition day. Things played in my hands today for a change. I got a few good breaks. With Lonnie driving, we ran about 10 miles up the lake through a blinding fog. We had to creep our way along the shoreline working our way up to my main river ledge. It took almost an hour to get in the vicinity of my ledge, but we couldn't take the chance of sitting out on the main river in the fog.

We opted to fish one of Lonnie's Carolina-rig spots, which was in the back of Mink Creek. We were able to find our way through the marker buoys and into Mink Creek. I really commend Lonnie on his ability to find his way. I've got a pretty good sense of direction, but I'm not so sure I would have been able to find it. We pulled up on a shallow, stumpy point that he had not fished in the tournament, (but he had caught fish there in practice). The point started real shallow and fell off into the Mink Creek channel, the perfect place for a Carolina-rigged lizard.

We were fishing blind in the fog. You couldn't see 30 feet. I was just basically throwing the same direction that Lonnie was casting. About the fourth cast, my lizard got a little heavy and I set the hook, catching a 4-pounder. Twenty minutes later, I caught 3-pounder. So I had a pretty good start.

A good keeper came shortly after that. Lonnie missed a couple of strikes. I felt really bad for him; he was having a bad day. I managed to catch every bass that bit.

After the fog had lifted, we ran back to my river ledge — only to find it was literally just covered up with local boats and the same pro I had encountered the day before. Two hours produced a 13-inch bass on a Rat-L-Trap.

Lonnie still had zero. I was able to detect a lot of tension. He was really behind and he was feeling it. I just basically tried to keep my mouth shut and fish hard and keep an upbeat tempo because I knew he was pretty upset. The last thing I wanted him to do was to start feeling bad for himself and possibly hurt his day or mine.

Lonnie Stanley took me to a schooling bass spot in North Sauty Creek — a very shallow, stump-filled flat. When we pulled in, I noticed Rob Kilby and Denny Brauer. Lonnie said "That's my best area back there. We can't go in on them." Kilby was in second place with 25 pounds from the day before. Lonnie was kicking himself because we hadn't gone there earlier.

I did manage to catch a small keeper bass off of the shoreline on a gold Rogue. Lonnie caught his first fish at 11:15 a.m. on a Carolina-rigged lizard on one of his windy points at the mouth of this little cove. We pretty much wore that area out.

We ran to the mouth of Brown Creek to some more Carolina rig spots — shallow humps that fall into the main creek channel. We hadn't been there probably 15 minutes when I caught my sixth keeper.

B.A.S.S. founder Ray Scott is an institution — and a lot of fun — on the weigh-in stand.

I finished out my limit with a 14-incher.

In the last 30 minutes we pulled up on one last spot that Lonnie had saved, (a shallow sandy hump with a couple of stumps on it). I tossed out a lizard between the stumps and immediately felt a good solid thump. It turned out to be the fish I was looking for — a 5-pounder. That enabled me to increase my stringer to 14 pounds, 15 ounces, moving me into the top 25 entering tomorrow's final round.

I think I've got enough things happening where I could really make a move into the top 10. Lonnie was good enough to say that I could re-visit any of his spots if I wanted tomorrow. But I feel more comfortable doing my own thing, fishing my own water my own way. I still haven't fished that clear water on the lower end with that Rogue, which will be a backup option for tomorrow.

I'm feeling pretty confident at this point. I've re-spooled a couple of my reels and worked a little bit on my tackle. Time for bed.

APRIL 17th

Final day of competition. The whole world fell apart today. Sometimes you come away from tournaments and you can't help but feel sorry for yourself. Sometimes you come away from them and you feel good. Sometimes you come away from them mad at the world. That's exactly how I feel right now. I just had a nightmare day.

I started out the day on the grassbed out in front of North Sauty. There was a good ripple on the water and partly cloudy conditions. Because it's the Friday before Easter, there were lots of local boats sitting out on my area.

I started my day by hooking about a 15-pound catfish with my Rat-L-Trap. I fought him around to where I could just about see him before he finally pulled off. Then I caught a short bass on a Rat-L-Trap. With so many local fishermen running the grassline in front and behind me with a Rat-L-Trap, I just didn't feel comfortable throwing the same bait. So I switched to slow-rolling the 3/4-ounce spinnerbait with a big blade.

The spinnerbait produced my first fish of the day — a 13-incher. It never ceases to amaze me that a fish that little can bite such a big spinnerbait, but he did. My partner, wanting to throw something different than me, began throwing a Carolina-rigged lizard — and proceeded to catch four bass (including a 5-pounder) before I got another strike (a 13-incher).

It didn't take a rocket scientist to figure out that this is the happening deal, so I grabbed my Carolina rig and joined him. But it was probably forty-five minutes before I had my first bite on the Carolina rig. It was a nice one — about 4 pounds. But he wasn't nice for long. The fish came loose as I was swinging it toward the boat.

Because it was early, it didn't really concern me much that I lost a 4-pounder. There was still time to pull it out.

By now, the wind was starting getting up just a little bit and I had two choices: run south and fish a Rogue around stumps; or go north to my big-fish creek and flip a jig. I opted for the long run north, which turned out to be regrettable since there was considerable boat traffic from the nearby ramp. It seemed like there was a boat on every bank up that creek.

I abandoned this area with no fish to show for my two-hour stay. It had been a bad decision.

The ride southward was punishing. The water was very rough. I'm so sore right now I can't hardly move. I pushed it as hard as I dared in that rough of water. My partner never said a word.

I pulled into a Town Creek and stopped on a little grassbed that had produced several bites real quick in practice. The wind was blowing so hard I couldn't even hold my position. I was limited to just drifting across the grass throwing a Rat-L-Trap.

That technique hooked a 2 3/4-pounder that I fought all the way to the boat. When I went to swing him in the boat, the Rat-L-Trap popped free and hooked me in the shoulder of my jacket.

With 55 minutes left to fish, I pulled up on a little stumpy point near the weigh-in site. My partner caught two fish almost immediately. Then I caught my third fish of the day on a Rogue. With 30 minutes left in the day, I pulled into another little stumpy area where the water had not been muddied and I caught my fourth fish of the day which literally swallowed my Rogue.

My watch informed me that I had about 12 minutes left to fish. I snapped my Rogue across a shallow stump when a large greenback came out from behind a stump, flared it's gills and took my bait into its mouth. At that point I really thought that there was my gift fish — about a 5-pounder.

I said "Thank you, Lord," and swept my rod sideways to set the hook. I tried to muscle the fish to the boat. I wanted the fish so bad in that last 12 minutes of the tournament, knowing that it was going to put me in the top 20, knowing that it was going to make me a pretty good amount of money, knowing that my frustrations were going to be kind of relieved after such a tough day. I pulled on the fish too hard and I tore the hooks lose and I watched a 5 pounder swim away. Disheartened, I fished as hard as I could the last 10 minutes before heading back to shore.

My pathetic 6-pound, 2-ounce stringer dropped me from 25th to 54th place. I ended up with a grand total of 32 pounds, 1 ounce — 13 ounces short of what it took to claim a check. I'm disappointed with myself, especially the way I handled that last fish. The 11 pounds of fish I lost would have lifted me into the top 10 and would have given me an opportunity to make the Classic going to the last invitational tournament. Now that's all down the tubes, but I still have a shot at qualifying for the Classic on the Top 100 tournament trail.

Winning Ways

George Cochran winning weight of 55 pounds, 1 ounce and Rob Kilby's second-place total of 48 1/2 pounds came on the same pattern — spawning bass in the back of creeks that were difficult to reach. The most productive lures were a 1/4-ounce brown-and-chartreuse Strike King jig with a moss green Bo Hawg Frog trailer on 10-pound test line and a pumpkin-seed-and-chartreuse tubejig rigged Texas style with a 1/8-ounce bullet weight and 2/0 High Performance Hook on 6-pound line. The jig was Cochran's choice when winds made the water dingy; the tubejig worked best when the water was clear and calm. The key, he said, was casting the lure past individual stumps and swimming it to the top of the wood where he allowed it to sit and twitch.

I'm not a happy guy right now. Just very disappointing. We're going to drive home tonight. We stopped at Burger King and grabbed a couple of sandwiches for the road. Diane's kind of staying out of my way. She knows how I get. I just don't really want to talk to anybody right now. I'm mentally and physically just mad, tired, exhausted.

It's just been one of those seasons, I guess. I don't really have anything positive in my mind at this time. I wish I did, because I really hate to go home being as negative as I feel right now.

Chapter 15

Progress... But Not Enough

Virginia Bassmaster Invitational
May 6-8, 1992
Kerr Reservoir

MAY 2nd

We spent last night in Charlestown, W. Va., with my grandmother who is 83 years old. She might not be around a whole heck of a lot longer. So I try and see her as often as I can. She always loves it when we come through. She's a big fan of my fishing.

We left there about 8 o'clock this morning to make the five-hour drive to Buggs Island. We're at the Super 8 Motel in South Hill, Va. I wasn't able to get a downstairs room, but I did manage to get one on the end. They don't allow dogs. So we've got to sneak Diane's little Maltese dog around so nobody sees him in the hotel room.

I spent a couple of hours working on my tackle for the tournament. Just checking everything over. We got everything put together tackle-wise and unpacked. We went to Pizza Hut right next door for dinner. I'm going to try to turn in early.

The weather forecast for tomorrow is mostly cloudy in the morning and clearing in the afternoon with breezy conditions. I will probably fish the lower lake, where the clear water is, tomorrow. The Sunday boat traffic is probably going to be up. I don't think I can get away from it anywhere. There's going be a lot of fishing pressure on the lake tomorrow.

The water is up 5 feet into the bushes. It's falling slowly. Water temperature is right around 70 degrees. The moon is on the up cycle, almost full. The fishing should be phenomenal if this lake is anything like it usually is.

MAY 3rd

First day of practice. I had a long day today. I started out by fishing in the Nutbush Creek area of the lake, staying fairly close to the boat ramp and fishing a lot of main lake points as well as the backs of pockets. I kind of skipped from outside to inside trying to figure out what stage the fish are in and what they are doing. I managed to catch quite a few good fish — one about 7 and I had a couple of 5-pounders on the outside main lake points by slow-rolling a spinnerbait through the hardwoods. Once it got bright the bites slowed dramatically.

I moved back into the backs of the pockets and flipped the big willow trees and the buck bushes. From what I can tell, there are very few fish in the backs of the pockets. Most of them seem to be relating more to the main lake or main coves .

I caught about seven or eight 14-inch (legal-sized) fish or better on a 1/2-ounce spinnerbait slow-rolling it through the main timber points. And I caught three or four other good fish in the 3-pound range flipping a black-and-blue jig on the secondary points about midway back in the coves.

There are a lot of good-looking bushes and willow trees in the back of the pockets that do not seem to have as many fish. The water is falling pretty fast — about 6 or 8 inches a day. That should put them out on the tips of those points or on those outside bushes. The changing weather, I'm sure, slowed it down in the afternoon. I didn't get near as many bites in the afternoon as I did in the morning.

I pulled out of the water at about 6:30 p.m., which gave me a 13-hour day. After showering, I headed for registration. We met with some friends of ours from Indianapolis and went to Sizzler across the street. We ate as quickly as we could. Got in bed pretty early. It's about 8:45 p.m. right now.

I'm going to get up a little extra early in the morning. I plan on trailering up river approximately 30 miles to the Highway 151 bridge that crosses the lake. I'm going to fish the upper stretches of the lake tomorrow and see what happens.

I know the water is very dirty in the mid-lake area. It's clearer above the bridge. It clears up again down by the dam. Visibility is 2 or 3 feet. In that mid-lake area the water is less than 6 inches of visibility from what I can tell.

I'm going try and run above that mud and fish pockets and coves off of the main river channel for pre—spawners or spawning bass up in the bushes. That's the plan for tomorrow.

MAY 4th

Second day of practice. I trailered up to the Highway 150 bridge and fished my way up to the head of the river. It's fairly easy to navigate right now because the water is up several feet. You can run places in this river that you normally couldn't run. About half a mile above the bridge, the water cleared dramatically. I was able to get into some really good water color with 18 to 24 inches of visibility in some places. The water temperature is pretty uniform. About everywhere I've been it's been 68 to 70 degrees.

I've been working my way from the main lake all the way to backs of coves and in the middle of the pockets trying to figure out where the fish are. Maybe they were a little bit different on the upper end of the lake than they were on the lower.

I found out that they're definitely not in the backs of the pockets. They're relating to main lake or major coves. Very few fish are in the backs of the coves because the water has fallen almost 8 to 10 inches a day. That's got to be the reason. They don't want to get trapped in that real shallow water in the back.

I had nine bites today. I shook several off, but I did set the hook on a few of them. They were very heavy fish, particularly in the main river section in the Dan River. I was fishing short pockets off the river, just running from one pocket to another. I noticed that the fish would be on the outer most buck bushes which is typical of what we've been finding. Almost every bite came on a black-and-blue 1/2-ounce Hillbilly Rattlin' Jig with a No. 1 Uncle Josh pork frog — just flipping it or pitching it into the outer most bushes.

The bass seemed to be holding in the center of the bushes. It was cold this morning. Very crisp and sunny and bright. That makes sense that the fish were in the center of the bush. I feel pretty comfortable that I can come up here and run these pockets.

Flipping a jig produced five pretty good fish. The only problem is that it is a long way up here. It's a commitment to come up this far. Tomorrow, I plan to fish Butchers and Eastland, a couple of creeks that are in mid—lake that I have fished in the past and done quite well in.

Buggs Island re-wrote the B.A.S.S. record book.

I'm going to make my decision on what I'm going to do in the tournament there. From what I can tell, fishing is pretty darn good on Buggs. We'll see what tomorrow will bring. It looks like the water is going keep on falling.

We grabbed something at Arby's tonight, watched a little TV and got in bed pretty early.

MAY 5th

Final day of practice. I got a lot more bites today, fishing this mid-lake area than I had anywhere else. I just about locked myself into believing that the fish are definitely relating to the main lake and secondary points in the major coves.

I spent the first two hours today in the very back of Butchers Creek and caught quite a few fish despite the rain this morning. It came down in buckets for about the first two hours and was very cold. Thank goodness it let up about 9 a.m.

At least it got partly sunny. I was able to dry out a little bit. It never got above 55 degrees today. I caught several small fish in the back of Butcher's Creek (in a narrow channel that runs through the flat in the back of this creek), but just couldn't get any keepers.

I began to move out towards the main lake, paralleling steep banks with a spinnerbait. I caught quite a few nice 2- to 3-pound fish and had a lot of other ones that I shook off. I put a piece of surgical tubing over the top of the spinnerbait hook to keep from hooking fish.

Any buck bush located on a main point or a secondary point seems to have a fish in it. They don't seem to be in the willows or the hardwoods as much as they do in those buck bushes on the outside edge of the points.

The forecast is for rain and cold tomorrow with some wind. I think the bites are only going get better as stable weather and cloudy conditions develop. We're not supposed to have any massive bright clearing skies or high-pressure systems.

The fishing should be pretty darn good. You're really going to have to catch them here. It's a five-fish limit with a 14-inch minimum. I think a guy will have to have at least 12 pounds a day to make a pay check.

It's going to take some pretty good fish to do it. I noticed in the afternoon, though, that I get more strikes by flipping a lizard than a jig. I downsized to 17-pound test line, a 3/16-ounce slip sinker and a 6-inch lizard for that clear water.

At the partners pairing meeting, I drew a fellow from Indiana. He's going to allow me to use my boat tomorrow. He's catching his fish in Eastland Creek and I'm catching the majority of my fish next door in Butchers Creek. That's the place that I have the most confidence in. I had probably 15 bites today.

He wants to start in an area that he feels confident in using a spinnerbait tomorrow. Then we'll fish most of my water later in the afternoon. I'd prefer to do it that way anyway.

Spent some time on my tackle tonight. Turning in. It's pretty late now. It's after 10 p.m.

MAY 6th

First day of competition,. Today went pretty well. It's a short run to Eastland Creek, about 6 miles up the lake. The wind was blowing real strong and we had 2-foot waves on the lake. It was rainy and overcast and very cold — the coldest it's been. I wore my gloves just about all day today. And it was very cloudy this morning.

We started off throwing a spinnerbait at 45-degree angles along a gravel bank with scattered buck bushes and willow trees on it. Ray caught the first fish, about a 2-pounder, off of a standing willow tree. We fished the spinnerbait for about another hour and never got a bite.

We moved to another area where willow points mixed with buck bushes where Ray had caught some fish in practice and started flipping. Ray was running my trolling motor and we were both standing on the front deck.

In the next hour, I caught three bass in the 2-pound range. Then we proceeded to the area where I had been catching my fish in the back of Butchers Creek and started my working our way out with spinnerbait. I could not get the fish to come out and hit a spinnerbait.

I caught one fish flipping in a bush that I had marked in practice, where a bass had flashed on my bait. That was a good sign. I had four fish by about 10:30 a.m. Ray still had his one fish.

By noon I had run a lot of the buck bush points that I had caught my fish on in practice, but had no success. The fish didn't seem to be in those shallow bushes anymore. With this cloud cover, I don't know why they wouldn't be there. The wind was making it very difficult to fish those points. So I started fishing small deep depressions adjacent to those points. Most of those depressions have one prominent willow bush in them with some buck bushes around it. If it got too shallow on the points from the water falling, I figured the bass might have gone to those deeper areas near the sides of the point. And that's exactly what happened.

That move produced four or five nice keepers for me, and Ray caught several in the next two hours (flipping that lizard into those willow bushes). I culled two fish.

The winds were so incredible that even Diane tries to help hold my boat during the weigh-in.

With about an hour left, I was just running and gunning those little pockets. That produced my biggest bass of the day — although I didn't catch it. When I flipped between the two willow trees, the line jumped and the bait swam out. A 6-pounder came up and thrashed around. It went around the boat and past the trolling motor. The fished seemed to be hooked well. Ray got down to lip her, but the bait popped out of her mouth. That was a real bad miscalculation on my part. In my mind, I debated whether I should have swung her in the boat right away. Maybe the thrashing around allowed the hook to tear a hole in her mouth.

I ended up with five fish weighing 12 pounds. Respectable, but the average catch today was a lot higher than that. Fiftieth place is 14 pounds. I am just amazed at the number of fish that came in.

Tomorrow I'm fishing with my old buddy Homer Humphreys from Louisiana. Homer and I have never fished together, but we've been friends for a long time. He didn't do very well today, so he's going to ride with me tomorrow. He says he has a few points where he thinks we can catch them on a spinnerbait early. From there, we can go to my flipping fish since we're fishing the same area.

The weather forecast is for windy, cold conditions and overcast skies. I don't think anything is going change.

MAY 7th

Second day of competition. I had a pretty good day today. I feel good about the way things went. A couple of little things could have gone better, but overall I feel pretty good about today.

We started on Homer's water with spinnerbaits because it was rainy and overcast. Most of the big stringers that were caught yesterday were caught on a spinnerbait. We began fishing some hardwood gumtree secondary points with a 1/2- or 3/8-ounce spinnerbait, depending on how shallow the water was. This water is still falling 6 or 8 inches a day.

The first point we hit, I caught a 2 1/2-pounder and then added one about the same size to the livewell 45 minutes later.

From there, we ran to Panhandle Creek and began looking for similar types of points. I caught a small keeper. Homer still hadn't caught his first one yet and was growing concerned. I didn't help his anxiety when I then boated a 4-pounder.

That gave me four pretty nice fish in the livewell. We just kept fishing the same type of points. Then we came across a wind-blown point that just had a hardwoods on a clay bank. It was a little off-pattern, but we just kept on fishing.

It was there that Homer caught a real nice one — 3 pounds or so. At the same moment, I hooked a fish that smoked towards the boat. I couldn't catch up to it. I never got a good hook into the fish and it pulled free.

We caught several other keepers in the next hour, but nothing real big. Then at about 2 o'clock we hit one secondary point where Homer caught a 4-pounder and I caught one a little over 5. He then caught a 5-pounder of his own

We both ended up with a limit. My five bass weighed 15 pounds, 14 ounces. Homer's limit weighed 14—3. We had a pretty decent day. But everybody else caught them pretty darn good too. I'm still about a pound out of the top 50, even though they're paying 74 places in this tournament.

I've caught 28 pounds so far. I need to catch them again tomorrow. Being in the last flight tomorrow, I will have a short day. I drew Rick Johnston from Missouri. Rick is having a terrible tournament. He's willing to ride with me and do whatever I want to do. He also made it very clear that he needed to catch enough weight to qualify for the Top 100 pro-am circuit next season. He estimated that he needs to catch 10 or 12 pounds tomorrow.

Quite honestly, I'm in a similar situation. I need to catch them pretty well to assure myself of a birth in the Top 100 trail for next year. I've never really been in that position before. But I'm also in a position where if I would catch 15 or 16 pounds, I would end up in the top 20 in this tournament and make a real good paycheck.

Tomorrow, I'll begin by fishing points on the lower lake, but those big-bass pockets way up the Dan River keep calling me.

We ate next door at Pizza Hut tonight. Diane is getting cabin fever already. She's seven and a half months pregnant. It's hard for her to be in one small room and do the same thing all day, everyday.

All I want to do is eat, spool my reels (which I do every night), work on my tackle a little bit and go to sleep. But she's real good about it. I just wish that it could be a little different. But if we're going to try to stay be together on the circuit, I guess it's just something she's going to have to deal with.

She's feeling pretty good for being this far along. She's getting big though. I don't think her condition makes her very comfortable.

Tournament Tip

Be aware of weather changes that might occur during your fishing day. Even the appearance of a slight bank of clouds or a sudden breeze can turn the fish on. If this occurs, be ready to change to a faster-moving bait like a crankbait or spinnerbait. The appearance of the bright sun should signal a switch to slower lures better suited for making a tight presentation to the cover. Quick changes like these can be the difference between success and failure.

MAY 8th

Final day of competition. At the end of this day, I have mixed emotions. Not a bad day, but it could have been a lot better. I just haven't been capitalizing on a lot of the opportunities I have had.

Rick towed my boat to the lake this morning, so Diane could have the van, which was really nice of him. As we drove, I could see he is very concerned about his situation and how critical it is for him to catch enough weight to qualify for the Top 100 tournaments for next year. It would mean a lot to his career if he could make the Top 100 events, including some major sponsor help.

Hopefully we'll both do well, I told him.

We started off running main lake and main cove points with a spinnerbait. The hardwoods, where we caught them yesterday, were just covered up with boats today. A lot of people knew what was going on and they were running that same pattern, which made it very difficult for us. Everywhere I went it seemed like there was a boat.

At about 9:30 a.m., I made a major decision. Without a fish in the boat, I decided to make the long run north to the pockets in the Dan River where I had some big-fish action in practice.

The skies were clear and it was getting sunny. I felt the spinnerbait had lost its effectiveness by now, so flipping a lizard was a better alternative.

As I ran under the Highway 150 bridge, I looked at the riprap and I knew that a lot of fish had been coming on riprap. I just had a feeling that maybe we should stop and fish the laydown trees along that riprap that forms the foundation for the bridge.

About the fifth cast, I caught a 4-pounder. Pretty nice fish. We fished the rest of the riprap for another hour and 15 minutes without another strike. It was just a fluke fish or a one-fish deal.

It's 11 a.m. now and we're due in at 3:30 p.m. We had to hustle on up. I pulled into a pocket where I had shaken a several fish off on a jig earlier in the week and caught one about 2 pounds on outer buck bushes. Then I caught a 2 1/2-pound bass. That gives me three fish.

These fish are right where they were in practice. I flipped behind a buck bush and I hooked a real nice fish — 4 1/2 pounds or so. I wrestled with him, but I couldn't get him out of the bush. So I went to him, but before I could get my hand in his mouth, the fish shook free. That was a real heart-breaker.

I caught my fourth fish about 45 minutes later on an outer, isolated willow bush. All these fish came on the same pumpkinseed-colored lizard with chartreuse tail with a 3/16-ounce sinker.

Rick still hadn't caught a fish at this point. He asked me "Once you get your fifth fish, will you give me a break and let me run the trolling motor so I can catch enough to make the Top 100s?" Although Rick was fishing beside me on the front deck, but with me running the trolling motor, I was getting the first shot at each bush. I understood his situation and agreed.

At about 12:45 p.m., I entered a pocket and I ran into Ron Shuffield. Ron and I are very honest and open with each other. He knows that I wouldn't lie to him and he wouldn't lie to me. He said he had about 17 pounds in the boat already and he caught them all in Bluestone Creek on a spinnerbait. He had only gone to these pockets trying to catch a big fish and upgrade his stringer.

No sooner had we talked about that when I caught a 2 3/4-pound bass to finish off limit. I immediately kept my promise and turned the trolling motor over to Rick, who quickly caught one about 2 pounds.

I asked Ron about running into Bluestone Creek to try to get Rick a couple of quick fish (we had less than two hours remaining). He said he thought that would be a good idea and told me the general area where most of the fish had been caught in.

Personally, I probably should have kept running these Dan River pockets because I was catching good quality fish and getting a bite every 30 to 40 minutes. I think upgrading my stringer wouldn't have been that difficult, but again, I had to do what was right for Rick.

Winning Ways

Louisiana pro Jack Hains scored 57 pounds, 4 ounces of bass. His winning pattern involved fishing a white 3/4-ounce spinnerbait with a silver No. 7 blade around sweet gum trees on shad-laden points. "I looked for points with sweet gums running out into the water, with any depth on them, and wind blowing on them," Hains explained. "That held true every day, but there were fewer and fewer of them every day as they drew the water down." The bass, he theorized, were holding along the outside edges of the roots of the sweet gum trees to ambush wind-blown shad. "Water washed out under those roots, making them perfect ambush points," Hains concluded.

When we reached Bluestone Creek, we didn't have much more than an hour to fish. The skies clouded up as Rick took the trolling motor and headed down a bank with a spinnerbait. He caught a 5-pound bass, which gave him a shot of confidence. Soon after that, he boated a 4-pound fish and a 3-pounder.

It seemed like the Good Lord just wanted him to catch those fish. It clouded up just long enough for him to catch three nice bass on a spinnerbait.

I finished the day with 12 pounds, which gave me 40 pounds for the tournament. I finished 53rd, which was worth $1,000. Rick's 11-pound, 12-ounce stringer was enough to lift him into the Top 100 field for next year.

After a spaghetti dinner and packing the van, we called it a night. We'll sleep in a little tomorrow before driving down to Lake Norman in North Carolina.

Norman is the site of the last Top 100 event of this season. And my last chance to make the BASS Masters Classic.

Chapter 16

The Last Chance

North Carolina Bassmaster Top 100
May 13-16, 1992
Lake Norman

MAY 9th

Lake Norman, just north of Charlotte, N.C., is the site of the last four days of the 1991-92 season — the Bassmaster Top 100 Tournament. It's been a long, tough season.

Thinking back on the year, it's been trying. There's no doubt about it. I can think of 15 different examples or instances of why this year was tough. Lock problems, breakdowns, lost fish, mental errors, not having the right equipment to repair certain problems during a tournament. Just a lot of things that I didn't do right this year and a lot of circumstances that just didn't go right. Weather conditions changing on me in mid-stream. Lack of adjustments, and so on.

But I've got to clear my head from such thoughts. I still have a shot at making the BASS Masters Classic if I can just put together four solid days here. I'm on the outside looking in at the Classic in the Top 100 standings. Fifteen Classic qualifiers were decided last week at Buggs Island. Twenty more will get a Classic invitation from the Top 100 standings at the end of this week.

Making the Classic is so important. It's the high-water mark for careers in this sport. It means a massive amount of national exposure and increases your credibility with sponsors. And then there's the money involved. Incentive clauses in my contracts would pay me $15,000 for just making the Classic.

And that's peanuts when you consider what it would mean to win the Classic. At the Classic, the top 35 pros and five amateurs in the country fish on equal ground and all have a shot at winning the biggest tournament of all. You can struggle throughout the year just to qualify for the Classic and then win it — and your cares are over for years. The more promotional-minded Classic winners have turned that victory into more than a million dollars in endorsements and speaking engagements.

It's the Indy 500 of professional fishing. And being 14 pounds out, I still have an outside shot at making my fourth Classic.

We're staying in a mobile home on the lake, which is real convenient. My boat is in the water, which will allow me to get a little extra sleep each morning. Today was spent on normal pre-tournament stuff like working on tackle, tidying up the boat, buying a fishing license and putting together some sort of game plan for the three practice days.

The water here in the mid-lake area is fairly stained. It's very clear down by the dam, I'm told. The river is supposed to be fairly muddy, which is very typical this time of the year for most of these southern lakes. Tomorrow I plan on fishing mid-lake areas. Since it is a Sunday, there will be a zillion pleasure boats on it. That's not going to be a whole lot of fun.

MAY 10th

First day of practice. Today was a very crowded day on the lake. My intentions were initially to fish the mid-lake area, but after a few hours of fishing here, the boat traffic became so heavy that I ended up going up the river. I did find one stretch of docks and bank where I was able to catch three or four fairly nice keepers with my partner, Richard Everett from Texas, who is fishing the amateur side of this tournament.

Because of the boat traffic, I made a snap decision. I usually don't change my game plan in the middle of the day, but I decided to run as far up the river as I could and fish my way back. I really believe the tournament will be won in the river. From everything that I've heard and all the reports, all of the big fish come from the river. That's where I plan on fishing the tournament. I'm here to win. If I'm going to make the Classic, I probably need a top-five finish. So I'm going to fish for the larger fish.

I ran up to the headwaters of the river where there is a dam and a power generating station. There's a lot of current. It looks a lot like Lake Wylie, located just south of here, which I fished last June. I caught some huge fish out of the river in Lake Wylie by flipping a jig where the laydowns broke the current. I tried the same thing for two hours today, but didn't have a bite.

As I fished my way downriver, I managed to catch two fairly nice fish that were in pockets just out of the current. The backwater areas are basically just inches deep — not enough water to hold fish. My only bites came from fish relating to main-river cover. It reminds me a lot of Buggs Island. I think the fish are doing basically the same thing. They're already finished spawning and have moved out of the backs of the coves.

I caught one bass weighing about 3 3/4 pounds — which is a giant for this lake from what I'm told — and another 2 1/2-pounder. I ended up with five or six keepers, all on a black-and-blue 3/8-ounce jig with a No. 11 pork frog.

Diane had dinner ready. Tied the boat up and put the charger on it. Locked everything up and walked right up to the house. Ready to turn in a little earlier tonight. It's about 9 o'clock and we're in bed.

MAY 11th

Second day of practice. I practiced today with a friend, Steve Tilly, an amateur from Tuscaloosa, Ala. He's rooming with us also. That made it pretty convenient. We got up about 5:30 a.m. and headed down to the boat.

We began upriver today where I left off yesterday and began working our way down the river. I fished the backwater areas for about the first two hours unsuccessfully. Then I started fishing main river blowdowns and willow trees. The willow trees were too shallow. I couldn't get a bite out of them. But I did start to get quite a few bites out of those main lake laydowns on channel banks and river islands.

I caught quite a few good keepers and shook off several other fish in an area that had some islands right in the middle of the river. There was a little bit of current moving around them and positioning the fish laydowns. Instead of flipping today, though, I backed off and dropped down to 14-pound test line for casting the jig. I also fished some main lake boat docks by skipping a jig underneath them.

It was very bright and kind of cool this morning. The fish

were tight to the cover. We managed to get 10 or 12 bites, which was quite a few for as tough a day as everybody else seemed to have. I feel pretty comfortable with things.

We fished until about 6:30 p.m., came in and went to Golden Corral for dinner. Then it was time to register for the tournament. At registration, all the ladies just couldn't believe how big Diane is getting.

MAY 12th

Final day of practice. I fished the lower end of the lake today. I had some cloudy, breezy conditions and thought it would be a good day to test out the clear water down there. I had heard lots of guys were catching fish down there, but most aren't keepers.

I started out by throwing a Pop-R the first two hours this morning on riprap and main lake rocky points. Although the Pop-R wasn't productive, I did catch quite a few fish on a spinnerbait and a gold Rattlin' Rogue around the docks. Probably caught 20 to 30 fish today and had another 10 to 15 follow the bait out from the docks. Nine or 10 were keepers. I was pretty impressed with the size. I had a couple of fish in the 3-pound range.

It's a pretty simple pattern. Even though it's the lower end of the lake, the fish are still on the outside of the pockets. The first two or three docks going into a pocket seemed to be the ones to key on. They had the most fish on them. But there needs to be at least 6 feet of water under the pilings to be productive. A lot of guys are fishing worms and tubejigs and things like that around the docks, but I can cover a lot more water with a Rogue. They seem to come out and eat it pretty good.

I think I'm going to start the tournament on the lower end. I'm going to try to catch a quick limit on a Rogue and then run up river to catch a big kicker bass on a jig. The forecast is for cloudy skies and breezy conditions tomorrow. It should be good fishing.

My amateur partner for tomorrow seems a bit nervous. Friendly, but kind of jittery. He just wants to stay out of my way he said. He says he's "just here to learn." You meet a lot of nice guys in these pro-am tournaments.

MAY 13th

First day of competition. A cloudy and windy morning. My plan was to fish very fast today and cover a lot of water. Fish as many docks as I can. Try and catch a limit early. But it wasn't quite as easy as I anticipated. We did get quite a few bites. I caught 30 to 35 fish today jerking a Rogue on 10-pound test Stren. But I just couldn't get the sizable fish to bite the lure. I had several of them flash at it.

The weigh-in line can be too long or too short — depending on the weight in your bag.

With the windy conditions and the clouds, I don't understand why the bigger ones wouldn't bite. Only seven of those fish were 14-inches or longer. My largest five only weighed 6 pounds, 7 ounces. Very skinny and emaciated looking. They had sores on them, which makes me think there's something wrong with this lake. I don't know if there has been any studies done on Lake Norman or not, but the fish are just terrible looking.

I may have made a bad decision by spending the entire day on the lower end of the lake. But it's hard to leave when you're catching those kinds of numbers and knowing that the next bite could weigh 5 pounds. That's what happened in practice.

My 6 1/2 pounds is just out of the money, but I'm not gaining any ground in the Classic standings.

Diane fixed hamburgers and hot dogs tonight on the grill. We all devoured them. My amateur trailer-mates didn't fare a whole lot better than I did today. But it's a four-day event and just about anything can happen in a four-day tournament. I'm going to run back downriver tomorrow and try to catch as good a stringer as I can. Hopefully, tomorrow I'll be smart enough to run up river in the afternoon to try to catch a good fish.

MAY 14th

Second day of competition. The sky cleared a little bit today. We didn't have quite as much cloud cover or wind and the fishing on the lower end was a little tougher today. I fished that Rogue around the docks, but ran some new water. I really believed the pattern I'm using would work anywhere.

So I fished all new water today. I think that was a mistake. I didn't catch nearly the numbers of fish in the new water.

I managed to catch four keepers by about 2 p.m. With less than two hours before I was due at the weigh-in, I decided to run upriver to finish out my limit — hopefully with a kicker. Fifteen minutes later, I was casting to laydowns in my main river island area with a jig. The bass seem to be positioned on the lower ends of the islands.

I immediately caught a short fish. Then I caught a 15-inch keeper, which gave me my fifth fish for the day. Another 15-incher culled a slightly smaller bass.

I noticed that the water is clearing dramatically up there. I don't know if that is good or bad. I think that water color puts the fish shallow, but the clearing water might drive them a little bit deeper and make them a little bit tougher to catch.

The final weigh-in at Lake Norman drew a huge crowd.

My five bass weighed 7 pounds, 7 ounces, giving me 13-13 for the tournament. That's just ounces out of the money, and I gained a little ground toward the Classic.

I'm going to turn in pretty early. It's only about 8:30 p.m. Everybody else is watching TV, but I'm whipped. Fishing hard for 11 days in a row is really wearing on me. It's obviously wearing on Diane, too. That's part of the reason I'm going to bed early. She says I'm not paying enough attention to her and I'm a little too much into what is going on. I've been awful quiet lately. I guess it's the winding down of the season. It's coming down to the end. It doesn't look like I'm going to accomplish what I set out to do. I don't think there's going to be a top-five finish here for me, or a BASS Masters Classic appearance in August. I guess it's really starting to soak in and it's not making me a very pleasant person to be around. But I'm doing my best. We'll see what happens tomorrow.

MAY 15th

Third day of competition. My weights are getting a little better each day. I had five fish today that weighed 8 pounds, 7 ounces. Although it moves me into the top 25, it's not enough to win this tournament or to move up dramatically in the Classic standings. But still, I am executing well and expanding my pattern each day.

I went back to my areas in the lower end of the lake where I caught so many fish the first day of competition. I continued throwing that Rogue around the docks and fishing a spinnerbait on the windy points down there.

But I started this day casting a Pop-R in those same areas and caught a 2 1/4-pound bass off of the back corner of a dock. The better quality fish seems to always hit that topwater bait. I fished a Pop-R an awful lot after that, but I just couldn't get another bite on it.

I just skipped around from dock to dock and point to point throughout the day. I caught most of my keeper fish late in the day — the fourth coming about 90 minutes before check-in. At that point, I made the 15-minute run upriver to the islands and picked up my jig rod.

There were a lot more boats fishing those islands today. Word must be out. I didn't get a strike on the lower ends of the islands, so I ran a couple of nearby points. I fished every laydown thoroughly, but couldn't get a bite.

With about three minutes left to fish, I pulled a 2-pounder out of a laydown. I only had time then to head for the launch site. That felt pretty good.

I've been improving my weight a little every day. If I can catch about 9 pounds tomorrow, I'll make the top 25 for sure — and feel like I've at least accomplished something these last couple of weeks.

My only chance of catching a big stringer tomorrow is throwing that Pop-R a lot more that I have so far. I think it will be my main bait tomorrow.

Diane fixed lasagna. Pretty good stuff. We are going to turn in at about 9 p.m. Everybody else is working on their tackle. I've got three rods with Pop-R, a jig and a Rogue ready. That's what I'm going to use tomorrow.

MAY 16th

Final day of the 1991-92 season. I started the morning by fishing a riprap point within sight of the take-off. Every morning, I had wanted to stop there, but it always had another boat on it. This morning I was the third boat out and I stopped there. I found that 3- and 4-pound bass were chasing shad completely out of the water near the tip of the point. I thought "this is my shot."

I began throwing a Pop-R right on that point and thought I worked it thoroughly, but didn't get a strike. So I turned and started up the riprap bank. My partner threw right in where I had just fished and caught one about 3 pounds. I turned the boat back around, made one cast and I caught a 2 1/2-pounder. The next cast produced a 15-inch bass.

It was fast and furious. It was also the only three topwater bites we had all day. We fished a Pop-R for almost two and a half hours trying to get one or two more strikes.

As I was heading for the next point, Randy Blaukat pulled up in front of me and caught a 3-pounder. Kind of ironic. If I had been a minute sooner...

I proceeded down to the south end of the lake to my dependable docks and points. But I didn't experience anything close to the action I had enjoyed before. The sun was out and the water flat. Just not a

very good Rogue day. I stayed after them, but I just couldn't make them come out from underneath the docks to hit that Rogue. I did manage to catch one that followed my Rogue out from a dock, by casting a 5- inch Kalin grub back into the area.

Due to the fact it was a Saturday, the boat traffic was just horrendous. I couldn't fish effectively. Every dock had people on it. With about an hour and a half left, I ran upriver to fish my island area. There was even more boat traffic there than anywhere else. I didn't catch another keeper.

My three fish weighed 4 pounds and 7 ounces. I missed the money by 2 pounds, 12 ounces. I ended up with a total of 26 pounds, 4 ounces for the tournament.

I finished the year in 43rd place in the Angler of the Year standings and 48th place on the Top 100 circuit. I missed the Classic by exactly 11 pounds.

I would like to think I learned a lot from my mistakes this year and from the few things that went right. The bottom line is that although I'm 43rd in Angler of the Year, I'm almost ashamed of it. There's a lot of guys out there that would be happy to have finished that high. But not me.

Winning Ways

Stanley Mitchell led this tournament from wire to wire on the strength of a shoreline pattern that produced 46 pounds of bass. His most potent lures were a chartreuse-and-white 1/2-ounce Stanley spinnerbait with silver No. 1 and gold No. 4 1/2 willowleaf blades; and a Super Floater straight-tailed worm without a weight (both on 10-pound test line). To coax a more subtle action out of the lure, Mitchell impaled a thin 1/0 long-shank hook through the middle of the worm, leaving the hook point exposed. He targeted spawning bass in 1 to 6 feet of water — covering as much wooden structure as possible.

Looking back on this season, I'm going to treat it as a real learning experience.

As I look back on it, it will probably be some of the happiest times of mine and Diane's life. The bottom line is that if this baby is born healthy, all of this fishing stuff won't seem quite as important. Compared to that, fishing isn't a life-and-death matter.

Ironically, the BASS Masters Classic is being held almost a month earlier than normal and Diane's due date is approximately on the first practice day of the Classic.

Chapter 17

Epilogue

It's been a strange summer for me in a lot of ways. For one thing, I've been home for almost three months, which is the longest period of time I have spent here in the past 10 years. I've had plenty of time to relax and reflect on a lot of things, especially, the events of the 1991-92 season — both on and off of the water.

But it hasn't been an uneventful summer.

While some of my peers have been spending time in Alabama preparing for and then competing in the BASS Masters Classic, I've been in the gym, lifting weights and running to get in shape for the 1992-93 season. And I've been doing some fishing as well — guiding two or three days a week on the Ohio River near my home.

It's given me time to really take care of the other side of professional fishing that most people never see — the business side. That means working with my current sponsors, pursuing new sponsors from outside of the fishing industry and planning my seminar schedule for 1993.

Missing the Classic was painful from a personal standpoint, but my sponsors are firmly in my corner. They understand that there will be more Classics for me.

The hurt of missing the Classic and enduring the past season was put into proper perspective on Aug. 27th at 4:15 p.m. with the arrival of Ryan Joseph Thomas, my first child. That 7-pound, 13-ounce boy will change a lot of things in my life, including my overall outlook.

Ironically, Ryan was born on the first official practice day of the Classic. While the guys were in Birmingham looking for concentrations of fish, I was in the delivery room for 15 hours coaching Diane through labor. And you know what, I wouldn't have traded places with them for any amount of money.

I believe that some things are just meant to be.

My other summertime activity has been bringing this book to a close. For the past year, I've made myself talk into a tape recorder at the end of every practice and tournament day — regardless of whether I felt like talking or even had anything to talk about.

Sometimes these recordings have been hard to do. My hope is that you, the reader, can get some positives out of my experiences of the past year. Learn from my mistakes. See where I made my adjustments or where I should have made adjustments.

More than anything else, I hope the weekend fisherman can relate to my experience, because, let's face it, we're not all Rick Clunns and Larry Nixons. The average fisherman has a lot more downs than he has ups. I just want you to know that even the top professionals have their tough times, too.

Diane made me realize that you don't always have to be a winner to be a winner. There is a lot of good that can come out of any year, even when you're not on top. The Lord has blessed me with a wonderful family and good friends and allows me to make a good living doing something I truly love. That in itself should be enough for anyone.

But still, I'm laying the groundwork for the 1992-93 season and itching to get back out there. It all begins again with the Bassmaster New York Invitational in September. Don't get the impression that I don't want to be a Rick Clunn or a Larry Nixon. I'm always trying to be the best that I can. I'm only 31 and I've got a lot of good years ahead of me.

Joe Thomas
Mainville, Ohio
Aug. 27, 1992

**My family responsibilities bring my life —
and fishing — into proper focus.**

Chapter 18

An Afterword

EDITOR'S NOTE: The pages of Diary of a Bass Pro originally ended with Joe Thomas headed for the St. Lawrence Seaway and pre-fishing practice for the first B.A.S.S. event of the 1992-93 season. He left his Ohio home in an atmosphere of optimism tempered with the frustration of the past 12 months. But as he attempted to put his disappointing year behind him and start the new year, Thomas' experiences in New York demanded a final chapter in this book.

I was fishing with a friend from Cincinnati, Pat Hailstones, and his 13-year-old son before the off-limits period for the New York tournament. We had planned to fish five days, but the wind blew so hard that we only fished about three and a half days. One of those days it was blowing real hard, but we decided to fish anyway. We went over to the Canadian channel.

We were trying to stay out of the wind as much as possible — it was blowing about 40 m.p.h. We eased into a little bay where there were a couple of boats tied up in an out-of-the-way place. I was throwing a spinnerbait and my buddy was flipping. I happened to look down in the water and saw a man floating. His hair was almost to the top. I looked at my friend and he looked at me, but we could hardly talk. I didn't want his son to see it, so I backed the boat out real quick and headed for shore.

I went and called the police. It turned out that the man had committed suicide. He had a rock tied around his leg and had jumped off of a dock. Actually, the water was pretty shallow. He had been in there for several days and, during their investigation, the police found his wife dead in her apartment. He had killed her. And the guy was also on parole for murdering his first wife 10 years ago.

I tried not to think of this incident being a bad omen for the season ahead. But I have to admit that it shook me up pretty good. I was by myself the next two nights in the hotel room and I saw it in my sleep. It really bothered me. I just got up each morning and went fishing — and tried not to picture that body in the water where I was fishing. It was kind of traumatic.

After leaving New York, I flew to Wyoming for my annual elk hunt. I didn't get an elk this time, but I got plenty of exercise and chance to clear my mind. That trip is always rehabilitating for me.

From there, I flew directly to New York for the Bassmaster New York Invitational Sept. 13-18. Despite my earlier encounter with the dead body, I was pretty psyched up about the tournament. To borrow a tourism slogan — I love New York. The Thousand Islands area of New York had given me three top-10 finishes the last few years, so it's easy to get excited about going back.

And considering the disappointing year I had during the 1991-92 season, it seemed like the perfect place to start the new tournament year — and my comeback — off.

During the pre-fishing period, I checked an area that has been good to me in the past. But it's not an easy place to get to. To get there, you have to cross more than 40 miles of open water (Lake Ontario) to reach this large bay. Until this tournament, I had never seen a tournament boat in this area.

It would take anywhere from an hour and five minutes with dead flat water — which I've only experienced here once over the years — to almost two hours when the water is rough (like it usually is).

Take it from me, this is a tough place to reach by boat from the French Creek Marina launch site. I have the confidence in myself and my boat to go out there in that dangerous water. But yesterday was about as brutal as you can experience in a bass boat. It's not so much the 8- to 10-foot waves that people tend to talk about; the largest waves I saw were about 6 feet. But I was running through 40 miles of open water and 4- and 5-foot waves. You have to concentrate so hard. You have to be right on top of your game. You can't let up for a second. Sometimes, I took time out just to rest. I had to stop and adjust my belt or the rib strap on my Yamaha life jacket and take a few seconds just to breathe.

It's so difficult to concentrate on each and every wave you encounter, but you have to. I only skimmed a couple of big waves. I hear of guys eating five and six big waves a day — that's just a lack of concentration. The whole key to running big waves is when they crest, come off of the throttle and ride the wave down. When the boat starts to pick itself up on the next wave, then you use the throttle. If you use the throttle on the crest or on the way down, you're asking for trouble.

My favorite area is a large, shallow bay (about 3 miles long and a mile across) on its extreme southern end there is an irregular grassline with several high spots in it. The grass basically rings these high spots. By watching my Lowrance X-60, I stayed on the edge of the grassline and pitched a 1/2-ounce jig on 20-pound Stren line into the grass, let it go to the bottom and bounce it a couple of times. If I didn't get a strike, I'd pick it up and move it.

I had one little section of this bay that had such a big concentration of fish in it that I got 11 bites in 45 minutes during the first day of official practice for the tournament. I dropped a marker buoy weight there and attached a plastic Gatorade bottle to it. And I literally fished within 50 yards of that buoy the whole tournament.

That area produced a total of over 80 pounds for myself and my three partners during the tournament.

What made it special was the fact that the area has high spots and the grassline is very distinct. It ends very abruptly. During this time of year, the bass always congregate on well-defined grass breaks — particularly largemouths.

I was fishing in 9 feet of water and the grass grew up to about 7. The high spots would come up to 2 or 3 feet of water. But we never fished on top of the high spots. I stayed in that 9 feet of water where the tall grass was. The high spots helped form that very distinct grassline. Everywhere else, the depth is all the same and the grass just scatters and trails out forever. And there was no distinct line. You could go through there and catch a bass every now and then, but it was nothing like the bam-bam-bam action I enjoyed.

The first day, I drew Jim Bitter. I think Jim trusted me, but he really didn't want to go that far across the big water. So we started the day off by fishing in the St. Lawrence River. Finally, at 10:30 a.m., I had a small limit of smallmouths and Jim only had two. So I convinced him it was time to make the big run. Within 45 minutes of stopping near that Gatorade jug, I had culled four fish and he had culled three. We caught 15 or 16 bass.

My first-day five-bass limit weighed 14 pounds, 4 ounces, which was good enough for 15th place (and a little more than 4 pounds out of the lead).

On the second day, my limit weighed 13 pounds, 7 ounces. On a day when the wind howled and the big water rolled, my weight was enough to rank fifth among the 300-man field.

For the final day, I drew North Carolina veteran pro Jerry Rhyne, a pairing that had the potential for conflict since he was in fourth place and I was fifth. Jerry had fish in the St. Lawrence river (well away from my best area), but he proved to be a complete gentleman. Explaining to me that his area and pattern was best suited for only one angler (he was targeting individual pieces of cover), Jerry instead elected to ride with me to my water in hopes that we would catch enough bass for my boat to produce the first- and second-place weights.

Working together, Jerry and I enjoyed a great day. His five bass weighed 12 pounds, 13 ounces, and my limit totalled 14 pounds, 3 ounces. When the scales had stopped spinning, Jerry finished fifth, while I ended up tied with Shaw Grigsby for second place with 41 pounds, 14 ounces.

All of my fish were largemouths, except for two 3-pound smallmouths I caught on stops to or from Lake Ontario.

I seemed to catch more fish than my partners during the tournament. I think that's because I was making more drops. They tried to finesse the fish more. The bass bit when the bait reached the bottom. If the fish wasn't there, I would get the heck out of there and fish the next spot. I was really moving through the area fast.

To score the highest finish of my B.A.S.S. career is satisfying for so many reasons other than monetary.

Sure, I appreciate the $22,000 (which included a boat) I won. But I had a pretty tough year last year and it feels even better to be back on track. This is a great place for me. This is the closest thing we fish on the tournament trail to home water for me. I feel real comfortable here. I'm always confident here.

I'm on a real high right now as I pack up my gear and head for the next tournament on the Potomac River. Practice begins in just two days. But I am as excited about fishing as ever.

The skies are blue again...

Appendix

Joe Thomas'
Career Statistics

Date	B.A.S.S. Tournament	Lake	Lbs./Oz.	Place
Feb. 23-25, 1983	Texas Invitational	Sam Rayburn	15	118
May 25-27, 1983	LaCrosse Invitational	Miss. River	6-3	56
Sept. 14-16, 1983	New York Invitational	Seneca Lake	5-1	96
Oct. 5-7, 1983	Missouri Invitational	Truman Lake	23-15	9
Feb. 29- March 2, 1984	Texas Invitational	Rayburn	16-13	79
March 28-30 1984	Georgia Invitational	Lake Lanier	8-10	108
May 3-5, 1984	Florida Invitational	Lake Okeechobee	15-12	169
May 30-June 1, 1984	LaCrosse Invitational	Miss. River	12-10	82
Sept. 27-29, 1984	New York Invitational	Hudson River	26-15	49
Oct. 17-19, 1984	Missouri Invitational	Truman Lake	2-11	169
Feb. 27- March 1, 1985	Texas Invitational	Rayburn	10-1	205
May 1-3, 1985	Chattanooga Invitational	Tenn. River	23-9	12
May 29-31, 1985	Florida Invitional	Lake Okeechobee	37-7	17
Sept. 25-27, 1985	N.Y. Invitational	St. Lawrence River	9-10	185
Dec. 11-13, 1985	Georgia Invitational	Lake Lanier	6-14	114
Feb. 19-21, 1986	Florida Invitational	Lake Okeechobee	24-6	64
March 19-21, 1986	Texas Invitational	Sam Rayburn	17-14	60
April 30- May 2, 1986	Missouri Invitational	Truman	27-14	13
June 4-7, 1986	Super Invitational	Tennessee River	4-14	142
Oct. 1-3, 1986	New York Invitational	Hudson River	10-15	184
Oct. 29-31, 1986	Florida Invitational	Lake Okeechobee	27-0	82
Dec. 10-12, 1986	Georgia Invitational	West Point Lake	8-4	74
Feb. 23-28, 1987	Megabucks	Harris Chain of Lakes	10-6	128
March 25-27, 1987	Texas Invitiational	Sam Rayburn	22-9	39
April 29- May 1	Alabama Invitational	Lake Guntersville	38-7	12
May 27-30, 1987	Super Invitational	Kentucky Lake	34-3	13

June 22-27, 1987 Team Champ. St. Lawrence River 29-13 33
Aug. 13-15, 1987 BASS Masters Classic Ohio River 9-14 8
Sept. 23-25, 1987 N.Y. Invitational St. Lawrence River 33-3 13
Oct. 14-16, 1987 Georgia Invitational West Point Lake 7-8 77
Nov. 4-7, 1987 Top 100 Pro-Am Lake Okeechobee 35-10 39
March 16-18, 1988 Texas Invitational Sam Rayburn 19-0 48
Apr. 13-15, 1988 Arkansas Invitational Bull Shoals 19-10 106
May 25-27, 1988 Alabama Invitational Guntersville 23-10 77
Sept. 21-23, 1988 Missouri Invitational Truman Lake 0-0 279
Oct. 12-14, 1988 Arkansas Invitational Bull Shoals 2-0 200
Nov. 9-11, 1988 Tennessee Invitational Kentucky Lake 25-0 23
Dec. 7-10, 1988 Top 100 Pro-Am Lake Okeechobee 32-4 28
Feb. 20-25, 1989 Megabucks Harris Chain of Lakes 31-6 17
March 15-17, 1989 Texas Invitational Lake Livingston 19-14 41
April 12-14, 1989 Nevada Invitational Lake Mead 18-11 32
May 10-12, 1989 Alabama Invitational Guntersville 27-15 149
June 7-10, 1989 Top 100 Pro-Am Sam Rayburn 30-3 39
Sept. 13-15, 1989 N.Y. Invitational St. Lawrence River 34-8 20
Sept. 20-23, 1989 Maryland Top 100 Potomac River 34-8 10
Oct. 11-14, 1989 Virginia Top 100 Buggs Island Lake 22-12 69
Nov. 15-17, 1989 Arizona Invitational Lake Havasu 5-15 80
Dec. 6-9, 1989 Alabama Top 100 Lake Martin 38-4 9
Jan. 24-26, 1990 Florida Invitational Lake Okeechobee 17-0 122
Feb. 12-17, 1990 Megabucks Harris Chain of Lakes 33-12 23
March 14-16, 1990 Texas Invitational Sam Rayburn 22-9 113
April 11-13, 1990 Arizona Invitational Lake Powell 11-9 119
May 2-4, 1990 Alabama Invitational Guntersville 24-10 138
May 9-12, 1990 Tennessee Top 100 Chickamauga 53-14 3
Aug. 23-25, 1990 BASS Masters Classic James River 16-10 19
Sept. 12-14, 1990 N.Y. Invitational St. Lawrence River 38-6 7
Oct. 10-12, 1990 Maryland Invitational Potomac River 23-15 34
Oct. 17-20, 1990 Virginia Top 100 Buggs Island 16-15 30
Nov. 5-10, 1990 Megabucks Lake Guntersville 75-9 6
Dec. 5-8, 1990 Alabama Top 100 Lake Martin 22-6 73
Jan. 16-18, 1991 Florida Invitational Lake Okeechobee 19-6 89
Feb. 20-22, 1991 Florida Invitational St. Johns River 12-0 118
March 13-16, 1991 Texas Top 100 Sam Rayburn 47-9 29
April 10-12, 1991 Alabama Invitational Guntersville 26-2 116
May 1-3, 1991 Missouri Invitational Truman Lake 32-11 11
May 8-11, 1991 Arkansas Top 100 Bull Shoals Lake 48-14 9
Aug. 22-24, 1991 BASS Masters Classic Chesapeake Bay 12-7 33
Sept. 18-20, 1991 Illinois Invit. Illinois & Miss. Rivers 2-2 176

Oct. 7-12, 1991	Megabucks	Lake Chickamauga	7-4	101
Oct. 16-19, 1991	S.C. Top 100	Lake Murray	14-0	95
Nov. 6-8, 1991	Oklahoma Invitational	Grand Lake	5-10	190
Dec. 4-7, 1991	Georgia Top 100	Lake Lanier	28-4	48
Jan. 22-24, 1992	Florida Invitational	Harris Chain	3-3	122
Feb. 19-22, 1992	Florida Top 100	St. Johns River	35-9	23
March 18-20, 1992	Texas Invitational	Sam Rayburn	30-15	48
April 15-17, 1992	Alabama Invitatrional	Guntersville	32-1	56
May 6-8, 1992	Virginia Invitational	Buggs Island	40-1	55
May 13-16, 1992	N.C. Top 100	Lake Norman	26-9	37
Sept. 16-18, 1992	N.Y. Invitational	St. Lawrence River	41-14	2

B.A.S.S. Career Statistics

Number of times in the money	35	44%
Number of times in first place	0	0%
Number of times in second place	1	1%
Number of times in third place	1	1%
Number of times in the top 10	9	11%
Number of times in the top 20	11	14%
Number of times in the top 50	20	25%
Number of times in the Classic	3	

Career Winnings	$144,731.80
Average per tournament	1,832.04
Cash winnings	$89,728.00
Merchandise winnings	$35,000.00
Cash Bonus	$503.00

Total Weight	1773-10
Total Entries	79

1991-92 Angler of the Year Standing 42nd
with 218 pounds, 2 ounces.

Tournament Checklist

Boat Preparation

Navigational lights and spare bulb
Fire extinguisher
Whistle or horn
Flares and flare gun
Floating cushion
Spare outboard propeller
Spare trolling motor and extra prop
Small tool box
Extra fuses/electrical connectors
Trailer lights
Trailer wheel bearings
Trailer tire wear and pressure
Trailer brakes
Check connections/switches on electronics
Anchor and rope
Check all exposed nuts and bolts
Charge batteries
Extra outboard oil

Personal gear

Two personal flotation devices
Two rain suits
Rain boots
Gloves
Goggles
Spare sunglasses
Sunscreen
Towels
Fishing license
Large plastic bag (for multiple uses)
Flashlight

Fishing Gear

Measuring ruler
Culling beam or digital scale
Marker buoys
Compass
Topographical maps
Waterproof map case
Pen/highlighter
Catch-and-release livewell treatment
Notepad or small tape recorder
Insulated cooler
Landing net
Extra bilge pump and aquarium tubing (as livewell
back-up)

Fishing Tackle

Rod and reels
Spare reel spools
Tackle boxes
Sharpen hooks
Monofilament line in 6- through 25-pound tests
Re-line reels
Fish attractant bottles

Pork rind jars
Miscellaneous aids: split-ring pliers, Super Glue, needle-nose pliers, scissors and reel wrench

Vehicle Preparation

Tire Pressure
Oil level
Check Fluids
Trailer hitch and ball
Trailer light connection
Battery chargers
100-foot extension cord with three-way splitter
Large tool box
Spare lower unit
Spare trailer wheel hub and grease

Secrets of America's
Best Bass Pros
By Tim Tucker
Senior Writer, *Bassmaster Magazine*

ROLAND MARTIN
RICK CLUNN
LARRY NIXON
BILL DANCE
HANK PARKER
GUIDO HIBDON
GARY KLEIN
DOUG HANNON
SHAW GRIGSBY
TOMMY MARTIN
KEN COOK
DENNY BRAUER
JIMMY HOUSTON
RICH TAUBER

Volume One of the Bass Pro Series

$12.95 postpaid

Secrets of America's
Best Bass Pros

By Tim Tucker
Senior Writer, Bassmaster Magazine

"A Fishing Lesson With Every Chapter"

Their office is the great outdoors. A sleek bass boat is their workspace. Instead of a briefcase, they carry a tackle box. Their tools are rods, reels, lures and the latest in electronics. They have a job that most anglers dream of.

They are today's tournament pros, the vagabond troupe of professional fishermen who travel the country in search of fame and fortune. In the process, they have taken bass fishing to an art form, the result of confronting every fishing situation imaginable.

You can take full advantage of their hard-earned fishing lessons through the pages of **Secrets of America's Best Bass Pros.** In these pages, the biggest names in bass fishing share their innermost secrets with Tim Tucker.

"Secrets of America's Best Bass Pros should be viewed as a rare opportunity to take a ride with some of America's foremost experts. Whether you classify yourself as a weekend fishing enthusiast or dyed-in-the-wool bass fishing fanatic, Secrets of America's Best Bass Pros is a guide to better bass fishing, a textbook offering the reader a better understanding of the intricacies of an often-times complex game.

"To his credit, Tim Tucker has translated these complexities into simple language easily understood by anyone who has ever spent time on the water in pursuit of America's most popular gamefish." Matt Vincent
Editor, B.A.S.S. Times

Volume One of Bass Pro Series

Send check or money order to Tim Tucker Outdoor Productions Corp.,

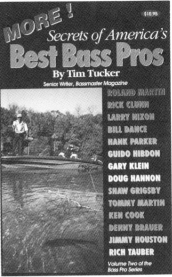

THE NEW
ROLAND MARTIN'S
ONE HUNDRED & ONE
BASS-CATCHING
SECRETS

Edited by **TIM TUCKER**

"… an outstanding reference work… offers a quick path to successful bass fishing."
— **U.S.A. Today**

"… a must for any bass fisherman's library. Heck, they ought to make a waterproof version to throw into your tackle box."
— **Western Outdoor News**

"No matter if you're a tournament competitor or a weekend angler, this all-inclusive guide will help fill the livewell."
— **Allentown (Pa.) Morning Call**

"One of the most informative books ever written on bass fishing… it would be hard to think of a bassing situation not covered in this book and each is covered in detail that make them easy to understand and copy."
— **Tampa Tribune**

"… the bible for hard-core bass fisherman."
— **Birmingham Post-Herald**

Hardcover book   429 pages

The New
Roland Martin's
One Hundred & One
Bass-Catching
Secrets

Edited by Tim Tucker

"The Bible of Bass Fishing"

Roland Martin may be the best-known fisherman in America. With 17 B.A.S.S. victories, nine Angler of the Year awards and 20 BASS Masters Classic® appearances (all records), he is certainly the most successful tournament pro of all time. Although some may not know it, Roland Martin is the father of pattern fishing, the way every modern-day fisherman — from the top pro to the weekend angler — has learned to fish. It was Martin who coined the phrase *pattern fishing* and defined it as a reliable way to locate and catch bass on a consistent basis. Now you can go fishing with the country's most knowledgeable bass fisherman through the pages of his new **Roland Martin's One Hundred & One Bass-Catching Secrets,** a 429-page book that has been called the most complete encyclopedia every published on the sport of bass fishing. Full illustrated, this book outlines the techniques and patterns that will produce bass on a consistent, year-round basis in any geographic region of the country.

"The book begins by revealing why bass strike, then outlines how water conditions combine with weather and tackle selection to increase your odds of landing a trophy lunker."
Bill Jobes, U.S.A. Today

$21.95 postpaid

Send check or money order to Tim Tucker Outdoor Productions Corp.,

Advanced Shiner Fishing *Techniques*

By Glen Hunter with Tim Tucker

Renowned Lake Okeechobee Guide Reveals His BIG-BASS Secrets

$9.95

"Your guided trip to the bass of a lifetime."

The wild golden shiner is the finest bass bait known to man. It produces more trophy-status bass than any other live bait or artificial lure in states where shiner fishing is practiced. But like all types of fishing, shiner fishing is most productive for those who understand it well.

In his **Advanced Shiner Fishing Techniques,** renowned Lake Okeechobee guide Glen Hunter outlines his complete approach to this exciting form of live-bait fishing. Not only will his secrets provide the insight necessary to catch bigger bass on shiners, any live-bait enthusiast will find that many of his tactics will enhance their success.

The allure of shiner fishing awaits discovery in many states. Shiners are native to most of the United States and southern Canada. And the sport of shiner fishing is about to explode with the publication of this book.

"Glen Hunter was one of the earliest pioneers of shiner fishing, who went on to become one of its innovators as well. As a guide, Glen is unparalleled... no other guide has promoted himself or the art of shiner fishing better than Glen. But the bottom line is that you cannot reach that plateau of recognition without accomplishing a whole heck of a lot on the water. He is the perfect candidate to write this book."

Roland Martin

"Whoever said live-bait fishing is simple is behind the times. Shiner fishing has developed into a real art where only the most skilled practitioners come out on top. This book, the first ever written on the subject of shiner fishing, is an absolute must for the angler who wants to catch bigger bass more consistently."

— Doug Hannon

"...wild shiners are by far the best bait for landing trophy bass. But knowing how and where to fish the shiners separates the men from the boys... the definitive guide to shiner fishing..."

— Tampa Tribune

"Thanks to this book... anyone can learn the secrets of shiner fishing."

— Gwinnett (Ga.) Daily News

"This book is the complete text on the subject of shiner fishing."

— Florida Today

$11.95 postpaid

Rt. 2, Box 177, Micanopy, FL 32667. Credit card orders call 1-800-252-FISH

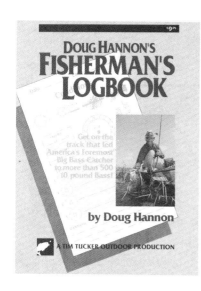

Bass Sessions
INSTRUCTIONAL AUDIO CASSETTES

Learn From the Pros:

√ In the comfort of your home
√ While driving to the lake
√ Sitting in traffic
√ Or fishing your favorite bass hole!

High-quality 30-minute instructional audio cassettes — a unique way to improve your skills as a bass angler! The country's top bass minds share their insights into specific areas of fishing in a conversational format that is both fun and educational.

The Bass Sessions Lineup:

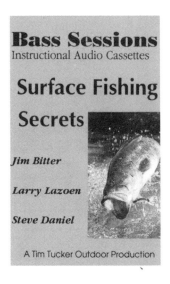

Bass Sessions
Instructional Audio Cassettes

Surface Fishing Secrets

Jim Bitter

Larry Lazoen

Steve Daniel

A Tim Tucker Outdoor Production

TROPHY HUNTING FOR BASS   **$8.95**
Roland Martin, Doug Hannon & Guido Hibdon discuss the habits and habitats of big bass.

CHAMPIONSHIP WORM TACTICS   **$8.95**
Gain insight into plastic worms from experts Shaw Grigsby, Jim Bitter & Bernie Schultz.

TUBEJIG TRICKERY   **$8.95**
America's three best tubejig fishermen — Shaw Grigsby, Guido Hibdon & Roland Martin share their secrets of finesse fishing.

SURFACE FISHING SECRETS   **$8.95**
Priceless topwater tips from veteran pros Larry Lazoen, Steve Daniel & Jim Bitter.

RIVER FISHING SIMPLIFIED   **$8.95**
Experts Doug Hannon, Bernie Schultz & Pete Thliveros on fishing moving water.

ADVANCED SHINER FISHING TECHNIQUES   **$8.95**
No one knows more about this art than Doug Hannon, Glen Hunter & Dan Thurmond.

Add $1 for shipping for each individual tape ordered.

Special Offer! Order all six tapes and receive a bonus tape Pro Bait Modifications free! All for $56 (includes shipping).

Rt. 2, Box 177, Micanopy, FL 32667. Credit card orders call 1-800-252-FISH

Get Your Free Copy!

Tim Tucker's

Bass Catalog

The finest in instructional books, videos, audio cassettes, gifts and choice tackle items specially selected by Bassmaster Magazine senior writer Tim Tucker

Name _____

Address _____

City _____ **State** ___ **Zip** _____

Mail to Tim Tucker Outdoor Productions Corp., Rt. 2, Box 177, Micanopy, FL, 32667

Learn From the Pros!